Before the 3 Rs

Before the
3 Rs

by
Mariann P. Winick

Illustrations by Ralph Wehrenberg

Photographs by
Regina P. Becker, Susan Savishinsky
and Mariann P. Winick

David McKay Company, Inc.
New York

For, my mother, a gardener
and my father, a builder
        one could not wish for more.

LIBRARY OF CONGRESS CATALOG CARD NUMBER: 72-86970
MANUFACTURED IN THE UNITED STATES OF AMERICA

Preface

Why bother about the intellectual development of preschool children, anyway? Won't that take care of itself? Isn't it enough to love them, give them food, shelter, and clothing; to keep them—and perhaps ourselves—happily occupied until it's time for them to go to school?

The answer, of course, is no. The child, for better or worse, is very much the father of the man, and if we want to see our children grow up into mature, complete human beings, we had better see to their intellectual nurture no less than their physical.

This book, then, is intended for parents and all those (teachers, day-care workers, play-group leaders, etc.) who feel they want to "do something"—but on the basis of valid knowledge of child development, and not at the expense of their relationship to the child. It is designed to help them "be with" their child and at the same time help lay a foundation that will enable him to profit later from his school experience. The core of the book consists of what I call reciprocal activities, which are based on a concept developed and field-tested over a period of ten years. For the concept itself I am indebted to the work of Harry Stack Sullivan, who felt that a robust relationship between parent and child during the preschool years involves, among other things, the evolution of reciprocal emotions, with both the parent and the child getting satisfaction and pleasure from the process of socialization.

The book, based on my experience as a mother and on my work as a university teacher and researcher in the field of child study, has two main parts: the first offers a platform from which to view some aspects of your child's intellectual development during his early years; the second describes and explains the reciprocal activities themselves. In the book, you will note, I use masculine pronouns. This is only because it seems more convenient than having to keep saying "him or her." No sex differentiation is intended; the material applies equally to boys and girls. However, each child is an individual in his own right, and each develops at his own pace. References to the age at which children "do" things—sitting up, walking, talking and the like—can therefore only be approximate and should be taken simply as signposts. Even children in the same family, with the same parents, same environment, same experiences, may do things at different ages.

"We have no art," say the Balinese. "We do everything as well as we can." You may feel the same way about bringing up your children. Inevitably, though, in your daily interchanges with them, feelings will sometimes be inappropriate or be misinterpreted. Parents are often told that their immediate responses to their children, especially their very young ones, are lacking in depth of emotion. Feelings of guilt arise. Am I giving him enough love? Am I fostering a sense of trust? Do I *emphathize*? Is he getting enough of my time? But you would not be the first by a long shot to harbor such feelings. Parents down through the ages have expressed concern about the development of the young.

Surely, there are no easy answers. Parenthood is not easy. No "course" can prepare you for it; no school offers a diploma. It is, indeed, a profession without a single professional or educational prerequisite, and the only training for it is on-the-job experience.

Mariann P. Winick, Ph.D.

New York, July, 1972

Introduction

To grow is to move toward independence, and ideally, the home is where this movement must take place, since the child's very sense of himself depends on the world he sees around him. Parents thus have the awesome responsibility of creating an environment their children can handle, manipulate, and—in some degree—master. This implies that parents understand and respect children's *right* to become independent. It is an implication, however, that does not always jibe with reality. For the fact is that many parents find it exceedingly hard to recognize such a right, particularly if it was not recognized by their own parents. The right exists, nonetheless, and what a child is really saying when he says "Help me" is "Help me to help myself." Doing it wisely is one of the most delicate and important jobs parents have.

Growing always presents problems. It means change, and change in children is unsettling. It comes, not at a steady, predictable pace, but in waves that overlap; often it cannot even be described. Still, we have relatively little trouble in accepting physical change, physical growth patterns. It is inner change that is likely to disturb us. We feel pride, naturally enough, when the baby takes his first step. We feel something else, though, something much more complicated, when we see him begin to move toward selfhood and independence.

Actually, the drive toward independence exists right from the beginning. The infant reflects it in his endless flailing and kicking. Independence feeds, as it were, on activity, on movement, and the infant's every waking hour is filled with it. Later, action becomes more purposeful. As the child grows older, you can see in him a self-directed effort to *do*, to accomplish, to be his own person. And one of the keys to this kind of growth is lovingness—tenderness—on the part of the parents. There can be no doubt that physical and psychological tenderness shown children at an early age is an essential ingredient in the making of truly human beings.

Toward infants, tenderness comes easily, called forth by their sheer helplessness. But before very long, soft cuddly bodies turn into tough, squirming bundles of resistance—as anyone who has ever tried to cuddle an unwilling two-year-old can attest. Does this mean that, at two, the need for tenderness disappears? Not at all. It just has to be expressed in other ways.

The need for tenderness is mutual. Parents satisfy it in their role as caretakers. With infancy left behind, however, a new necessity emerges. The mother or father, or both together, must begin to serve as socializing agents, guiding the child into acceptable ways of behavior, of interacting with others. The parents' own tender, cooperative behavior of yesterday ends. Earlier patterns of reciprocal activity—cuddling, cradling, rocking, feeding, bathing, diapering—give way to new ones

such as storytelling, reading, playing games, taking a
walk. An unaccustomed word—No—comes into greater
and greater use. For the mother, life becomes more
hectic, more wearying, even depressive. In her new role it
becomes more difficult for her to show the tenderness
her child needs—it's hard to say No and feel tender at the
same time. Moreover, her child now feels an additional
need: not only to receive tenderness, but also to give it as
well. How fully his needs are met depends on the extent
to which the parents' socializer role is allowed to displace
their caretaker role.

But the two roles—played more and more these days
by both parents, not just by the mother—are not
incompatible. The home need never—should never—
duplicate the school. You can successfully play your part
as parent without becoming a teacher intent on extract-
ing an excellent performance from your student. It is true
that the Montessori Method, introduced by Maria Montessori, the great Italian educator (and, incidentally,
Italy's first women medical doctor), has been enjoying a
considerable revival lately. But many parents have mistaken its principles and have permitted themselves to be
seduced into the role of substitute teacher. The books
and articles proliferate: *Teach Your Child to Read, Teach
Yourself and Your Child the New Mathematics, Make
Your Home a Science Laboratory, Raise Your Child's IQ.*

There are serious dangers in such a fusion of roles.
The parent's role is necessarily eroded, and the child,
with good reason, may neither be able to maintain
himself as both child and student nor accept his parent as
both parent and teacher. There is the danger that distrust
of teachers and formal education, implied by the parent
when he assumes a teacher's role, may be conveyed to the

child, to the detriment later of his school career. Finally, there is the danger that parents, who in fact do have a legitimate role as educator, may neglect it in favor of trying to teach such specific skills as reading and writing. Thinking is by far the most important process engaged in by man. We rejoice when we see the first rudimentary signs of it in our children. Intuitive thinking, however, is not a mystical or a metaphysical process. It is based on the ability to integrate words, actions, and concepts, and it can be developed. Its origins can be found in the earliest stages of infancy; it is intimately related to feelings of tenderness and trust inspired by the parents. So when parents become taskmasters, it's no wonder that children are confused and distressed. The real function of the home is to serve not as a school but as an environment planned and managed in such a way as to enable the infant to grow into childhood and eventually into the world of words and ideas with a substantial reservoir of experience and the ability to transmute experience into activity.

Dr. Montessori herself was not interested so much in promoting a particular method of education as in advancing a theory of instruction. Her goal was not the creation of highly "intellectual" facile adults but the cultivation of true humanitarians prepared to be activists in life rather than passive victims. Long before most, she recognized the incalculable value of specifically fostering not only the motor skills of children but their sensory development as well. On this, in fact, her entire structure rests. She cautioned, however, against confusing the "education of the senses with the concrete ideas which may be gathered by *means* of the senses." (Italics added.) The true aim of education, she said, is "to develop the energies." But energy must have outlets or it creates chaos; the "buzzing, blooming confusion" John Dewey mentioned overwhelms the child.

This, then, is the role of the parent: to provide a quality of living and life that gives sustenance for growth.

You're lucky. As a parent, you have what every teacher envies: time, space, and a limited audience. You are in the best possible position to help your child become the person he *can* be.

More than seventy years ago, writing about the early loss of selfhood, Dr. Montessori said:

> How can we speak of Democracy and Freedom when from the very beginning of life we mold the child to undergo tyranny, to obey a dictator? How can we expect democracy when we have reared slaves? Real freedom begins at the beginning of life, not at the adult stage. These people who have been diminished in their powers, made short-sighted . . . , whose will has been broken by elders who say: "Your will must disappear and mine prevail!" How can we expect them, when school is finished, to accept and use the rights of freedom?

Our young people throughout the nation and the world are asking the same rhetorical questions today.

Part I

Part 1

Contents

Early Development

Sensitivity

"Make the body capable of doing many things," said Spinoza. "This will help you to perfect the mind. . . ."

Training in elementary awareness—in developing the physical senses: sight, hearing, smell, taste, touch—is a task for the home as well as the school. Parents often lose sight of this. They are so bemused when their children begin to form words that they tend to overlook the nonverbal elements in their children's development. But the verbal and nonverbal are both important, and it's the parents' job to maintain an environment in which the child can have valuable experiences of both kinds. Seeing and hearing and touching are just as valuable as talking.

Perception, indeed, is basic to all mental processes. The mode by which we perceive the world—receptive, stereotyped, conceptualized, unconceptualized—largely determines the way we think. It follows, then, that if our perceptions are distorted or limited, life itself is dimin-

3

ished for us, dulled by inadequate thinking and inappropriate feelings.

Of the five senses, sight is perhaps the dominant one both in early and later life. Children are natural watchers and receivers. They are constantly taking in impressions and storing them away for future use. Long before an infant can clutch the world to himself with his hands, he grasps it with his eyes. This kind of experience, in watching and receiving, heightens a child's sensitivity and increases his intelligence. It helps propel him toward an active rather than a passive part in life because life is made rich, fresh, significant, not something merely to be endured.

A life dependent solely on the eyes for perception, however, is as seriously limited as one that depends only on words. The other senses must come into play. As the infant's eyes move toward things, his hands move, too, his fists opening and closing. He discovers his toes and reaches for them. Fingers feel, push, pull, explore. Movement becomes an essential part of sense perception. The baby moves his fingers to manipulate and touch, just as he examines things he can't reach by following them with his eyes. And everything within reach, of course, has to be tasted.

All this is of a piece, part of the slow process of maturation. At first the child depends entirely on perception and movement. Gradually, he comes to depend more on thought. The various bodily systems that meanwhile are developing—bones, muscles, nerves, and so on—all help to create the entity that is "me". By the time a baby is five months old he has in fact worked out a pretty fair idea of "me," and even of "me" in relation to

time and space. He can locate objects and can differenti-
ate himself from his environment. He can, for example,
distinguish between the bottle and his own hand which is
holding it. Make no mistake, this is a very complex
mental operation. In psychological terms, it involves the
recognition of different characteristics, separating them
well enough to attribute them correctly to the two
objects, and making the difference observable and functional—that is, the baby knows enough to reach deliberately for the bottle and put it to his lips, or push it aside.

The act of sensing is, in a way, a form of thought.
And as the child's perceptions become keener and his
sensory experiences are more numerous and more complicated, it becomes quite clear what an enormous contribu-
tion they make to his intellectual development.

Movement: The Thread of Thought

Movement, too, is a form of thinking: thinking made
visible. In infancy, the two acts are simultaneous: to
think is to act. When the infant wants attention, he drops
his rattle out of the crib. Physical movement is also a
teacher. The child learns by moving. Toddling about,
carrying things, tripping, crawling, walking, he is always
adding to his knowledge. Layer by layer, he keeps
building up his supply of information about himself and
his environment. He constructs mental models of everything—people, places, things, time, space. Testing one
piece of information against another, he constantly
changes the models as he goes along. In the developmental process, movement is thus nòt only an outward
manifestation of thought, but also its medium as well.

The child who *moves*, therefore, is likely to be physically and mentally more mature than the passive child, although physical maturity and chronological age are at best only rough indices of intellectual maturity.

At home and in school, frequently, movement is consciously or unconsciously interpreted as "threat." We restrict a toddler's movements around the house because he might bump himself or might sweep a treasured vase off the table. So we say, at least. The real reason may be something else. We may in fact be guarding against what we perceive as a threat to our privacy. The child's movements disturb us, or disturb our adult sense of order. On quite another level, the older generation today feels similarly threatened by the movements of the younger generation.

Yet movement is a vital element in the child's struggle to develop his powers and, within reason, it should be given the freest rein possible. No one in his right mind would think of blindfolding his child or putting stoppers in his ears. But we think nothing of confining a child to his room or keeping him in a playpen long after it has served its original purpose. A blind person or a deaf person can sometimes compensate for the loss of one of his senses through a sharpening of the others. What substitute is there for freedom of movement? How can one compensate for *its* loss? The child who is restricted in his movements, whose explorations are curtailed—whether physically or intellectually—soon stops exploring. Inhibition and restriction can lead only to a restricted sense of self and a narrowing of horizons.

Movement achieves functional unity between thought and the outward aspects of thought. An eighteen-month-old baby facing the problem of going down a flight of stairs for the first time, for example, relates bottom and top and makes the (to him) momentous connection. Gripping the banister, he descends carefully, planting both feet firmly on each step as he goes. By the age of three or four, the whole thing is, of course, automatic. But throughout life movement is an indispensable accompaniment to intellectual growth. This is why a child must find it possible to move about freely in his environment—city or country, suburb or slum—or else risk stultification.

Language: the Matching of Reality

Learning to talk has always seemed an effortless, unmotivated activity based on instinctual imitation. Only in recent times have we come to realize that it is one of man's most complex and most remarkable feats, and, while imitation plays an important part in it, we now know that it is not instinctual but a long, deliberate learning process.

The infant begins by imitating his own sounds made at random: grunting, crying, and so on. By his third or fourth month, the sounds are more specific: he is cooing and gurgling. In the following months, he begins to imitate *your* sounds. At ten months or so imitation is a serious part of the business of learning language, and you can pick out a word now and then. But also by the tenth month a new element has been added. We call it "matching," and it is based on the child's growing desire to experience *pleasure.* At this stage, the child actively enjoys matching words to real things; the motivation no longer rests on the impulse to imitate but on the pleasure principle. Recent studies in child development show, also, that not only is imitation itself a developed faculty, but so too is the pleasure experienced by children in "matching" and in language in general. It is a learned process which grows and matures through constant repetition.

One function of language is to structure observations and actions so that they are meaningful to the child. Naming things, for example, is the child's way of giving "being," through the magic of a word, to something he doesn't yet understand. He takes great delight in learning the name of an object—"apple," "bus," "dog," or whatever—and repeating it endlessly, doubling and redoubling his pleasure. He may drive you batty, but don't discourage him: his constant chatter is by no means idle. He is hard at work making the unfamiliar familiar, reaffirming newly acquired knowledge and shoring up confidence in his ability to handle language. Like any normal, healthy child, he is moving into the world by seeking pleasurable experiences. The more good talk he hears at home, the greater his pleasure and the firmer his step. The child who hears little or no conversation, on the other hand, may be facing a language barrier difficult to surmount later on.

But speech—or, rather, glibness—should not be *over*-valued. Speech is often considered the "true" barometer of thought. The two are, of course, closely related. However, because the development of speech is observable and obvious, its importance as a measure of thought and intelligence is often exaggerated. There is a vast difference between expression of thought and mere verbalization. Children, for example, parrot television commercials without any thought whatever. If you're caught off guard you can easily fall into the trap of mistaking patter for the real thing: "I can't eat my spinach," says a small boy in a magazine cartoon, "I'm suffering from the discomfort of an upset stomach due to excessive acidity."

The child, particularly the eight-to-eighteen-month-old, is not very discriminating about the quality of the speech he imitates. Give him good talk—in content as well as in diction and usage—and he will imitate it. Give him poor talk, and he'll imitate that. He's not fussy. And as between speech emanating from the television set and that spoken in the same room by a human being, give him the human being every time. Television talk doesn't have nearly the same pull on him in terms of his desire to enjoy it.

The preschool period, then, is both an "absorbent era" and an era of maturing needs. The child is assimilating a tremendous amount of information and knowledge. Meanwhile, his psychological and physiological needs are growing and must be met. How? By providing a wide variety of sensory, motor, and intellectual experiences. To be fully effective, moreover, these experiences must have "quality." The talk of a living, breathing adult, for instance, has it; the television voice does not, because there is no opportunity for reciprocal interplay. The experiences must also be reinforced, and this is done through repetition. When the child repeats a pleasurable act or word over and over again, he is, in effect, revealing intellect at work. More than that, he is moving toward the world by calling into play many different physical capacities as well. He is creating a mode, and it is this act of creation, this movement toward "matching," if you will, that gives him pleasure and makes further progress possible. In all of this, movement of both kinds—physical and intellectual—is basic. If parents could but picture early childhood as a time of *motion,* they might be better able to see it for what it is: an intense affair with living.

Fantasy: Unspoken Reality

Fantasy plays a large part in the life of a preschooler and it has very positive values for his development. An audience, however, is essential—more than that, an audience that *participates.* This is a profound need of the young child and he goes about fulfilling it with notable determination. Parents and older siblings are likely to see him as a kind of tail, always tagging along behind, always around, looking for something to do or "helping" mother in the kitchen. Actually, he is demonstrating his need for an audience, and, in their day-to-day as well as long-range planning, parents should take this need into account.

The way in which parents respond to the need is important. Researchers have observed two fairly common extremes of behavior, both of them to be avoided. There is the parent who all but literally pushes his child into the adult world, mainly through the use of words far beyond the child's emotional or intellectual grasp, producing confusion. And there is the parent who throws himself into the *child's* world, again with words—baby talk. In both cases, it is the *parent's* need for an audience that seeks gratification. He becomes the performer, the star. The child is really being ignored. *He* becomes the audience—and a captive one at that.

Mimicry of adults is another way in which children indicate their needs for self-expression. They make models of the people closest to them and imitate their phrases, gestures, and attitudes. Unable to draw a clear line between reality and fantasy, the child sees himself as the adult. He "drives" the car, takes care of the "baby," does "housework," builds "bridges," runs "trains." Fantasy objects may be real enough, only the child may not yet have run across them. His universe is still new and shiny, a constant scource of wonder and stimulation, but he has so far discovered only a tiny part of it.

Children literally cry out for contact with people and things. They make up little songs as they move about, and enjoy hearing an adult pick up the tune. Their dances are creative attempts to communicate something they are discovering about their bodies, and they want everyone to see. When a child seeks out an adult and performs some exercise of body or word, he is saying, "Look, I am like you!"

Fantasy at this stage is creativeness, not a creation itself. It represents movement toward reality and as such it should not be discouraged. The child dressing up in his parent's clothes, for example, is being creatively "fantastic." He is assembling bits of adult clothing in a "fantastic" way, and whether or not they fit is unimportant to him. What *is* important is the new picture of himself that he sees. The little boy sees himself as being like his father; the little girl in her mother's gown looks in the mirror and sees her mother. This kind of fantasy is an aid to growth. Only later on, when, as the result of negative experiences, the child uses fantasy as a means of escaping reality, of retreating into himself, is it any cause for concern.

The Child in Profile

During the first two years of life, the child lays the foundations for building his motor and sensory skills. He has begun to talk. Babbling has turned into recognizable words—words, incidentally, which the child may understand long before he is ready to say them, and contrariwise, may say before he understands them. By the age of two the child is the participant-observer. He watches the world with a knowing keenness. You can almost hear his mind ticking over. Until now, much of what he has taken in from the environment has remained largely inside his head; relatively little has been externalized. But now he begins to put his stored-up knowledge to use. He becomes completely attentive and can actually focus on everyday things. He truly turns pumpkins into coaches.

At two, the body becomes an important vehicle for learning. The child has been testing it up to now, plumbing its capabilities. Now he deliberately puts his body to practical use. He holds things and carries them about with a semblance of adult competence. A favorite activity of his now is having a party for his dolls and animals. The party is a creation, a means of enabling him to construct a world of his own ordering.

About this time, a serious question arises: toys. Should they be selected according to the child's sex— dolls for girls, dump trucks for boys, and never the twain shall meet? This really would be unfortunate. It would deprive boys and girls, both, of many pleasures. Boys often enjoy dolls and girls often enjoy dump trucks, and there's no good reason why they shouldn't. Children at this age are too new in the adult world to respect toy segregation by sex. They are simply not interested in adults' sense of "propriety," only in toys that move, make noise, and do things, or that they can do things with. A good selection, for play, companionship, and exploration, might include, in addition to dolls, stuffed animals, blocks, pull and push toys that make noise, a tricycle, a pedal-driven car, puzzles, things to take apart and put together. But remember, toys are secondary. If a child did not have a single toy bought in a store he would not be at a loss for playthings because his environment is full of them: water, stones, dirt, grass, trees, steps, rugs, boxes, spoons, pots, pans, cans, cartons, light switches— the list is endless.

By three, the child is entering "middle age," and the differences between him and his two-year-old self are considerable. At two, he enjoyed an activity more for the sake of his own involvement in it than for the end product or goal. He ran around the yard or park, aimlessly gathering leaves and kicking piles of them from place to place. The three-year-old, on the other hand, decides on a central dumping ground, brings all his leaves to it, and makes a single pile. *Then* he may choose to jump into the middle of it and kick it apart, or he may seek approval for having done such a fine job of collection.

Even when he has siblings either younger or older than himself the two-year-old has a close relationship with his parents. Because of it he has difficulty in handling his dependence-independence feelings. He would like to dash off, but he still needs the reassuring adult to approve. So he often prefers to play in a familiar place, by himself or with one friend, rather than join a larger group. However, the two-year-old is a sharp observer of other children and their activities. This is the greatest source of motivation for many children. They base much of their indoor activity, for example, on what they have seen outdoors: "shopping," taking "care" of the doll, building a "house," collecting "garbage," going for a "ride." By the time he is three, a child will play "follow-the-leader," where, at two, he was more likely to tease and push the leader instead of following him.

While "two" is a time of activity for its own sake, "three" is marked by testing. This involves not only observation, but exploration, experimentation, and the formulation of conclusions and new ideas. On an elementary but nonetheless real level, it is the beginnings of scientific methodology. Testing, at three, also involves other people as well as inanimate objects. By now, though, Junior has worked some things out for himself, and his parents find it less necessary to say No so often. He walks with a firm, sturdy tread, his back straight, his stomach flat, his chin up. Suddenly, one day, perhaps with tears of happiness welling up in your eyes, you realize that all traces of infancy have vanished.

Some child specialists feel that language—a bigger vocabulary, better sentence structure—marks the difference between the two-year- and the three-year-old. But this isn't the whole story. The child has been a listener and a decoder from birth. He has accumulated a vast nonverbal vocabulary of gestures and sounds. What has happened is that, by three, his period of complete physical dependency on adults has ended. The movement toward full physical and *emotional* independence is well under way.

The four-year-old—a "pioneer," experienced—now enters a new period of "creative pleasures." It's no longer enough just to be able to do something. What he needs now is to enlarge, to manipulate, to change the forms he knows into new forms. The words "his" and "theirs" take on meaning. The "I" that glibly falls from his tongue becomes the real "I" of the inner self. His need for emotional involvement is more urgent than ever, and he is fascinated by dramatic play. He has an absorbing interest in stories with whose characters he can identify.

In group play, he and his companions create very elaborate structures, both figurative and literal. He now sees and observes adults as apart from himself. Yet with ease he can become workman, ball player, teacher, or one of the big fellows. "Four" has enough bodily skill and experience by now to know exactly what his feet, legs, arms, and fingers can do for him. His energy seems boundless. He is always on the go, but it is at this stage of large-muscle development that he comes to learn how to sense his own limitations.

As he approaches five, the child realizes that fingers and hands have great power. The spoken word, also, is now within his reach as a tangible tool. Reading and writing are now possible. And the first key to both of these skills is simple: If the child enjoys saying words, hearing stories, talking in sentences—not TV commercialese; if he moves with coordination, likes to work with his hands and fingers, and is able to stick with an activity for at least ten minutes, then he is probably able to begin. But each child is different from every other child, and teachers and parents must judge for themselves when the right moment has arrived.

The five-year-old is his own taskmaster, and he's a hard one. He demands high standards of workmanship from himself. Numerical values now assume reality. Distance, time, quantity are investigated, related, and manipulated in a rather precise way. Interest in such things begins at the three-year-old level, grows during the fourth year and blooms during the fifth. The following pages contain a condensed outline of various aspects of the preschool child's development, divided roughly into three stages: infancy, from birth to eighteen months; early childhood, from eighteen months through the age of four; and late childhood, from five to seven.

Developmental Models

Self

Infancy

Great dependence; beginning of self-awareness; physical and emotional need for others.

Early Childhood

More independent physically, but still dependent on adults for emotional needs.

Late Childhood

Movement toward peers and other children of different ages, leading to reduced emotional dependence on adults.

Self and Others: One to One

Infancy

Basic feelings of trust and affection, produced by relationship with mothering one; physical handling and emotional climate influence levels of response.

Early Childhood

Begins to return affection; to share it with siblings and family. Beginning of trust in what parent says.

Late Childhood

Movement toward peers; sharing; wants to help and be helped.

Self and Others: One to Many

Infancy

Awareness of both moving and stationary objects, leading to differentiation between humans and things; familiar distinguished from unfamiliar. Mother is one main social figure but other relationships appear: daddy, granny, brother, sister, etc.

Early Childhood

Desire to be with or relate to peers (i.e., through sandbox, nursery school, etc.); realizes that family group includes more than self and mothering one.

Late Childhood

Discerns difference between world of children and "over-world" of adult; move to "groupness" resulting in emulation.

Inner Self

Infancy

Rudimentary awareness of dependence—feeding, toileting, etc.; begins to adapt to schedules and to desires of others.

Early Childhood

Rudimentary but developing interest in following commands and directions; child begins to set his own rules in absence of adult demands.

Late Childhood

Rules and expectations are related to many more
situations, particularly those involving other children. Right and wrong frequently decided on by the
group; sometimes questioned by individual children.

Inner Self and Physical Self

Infancy

At this level the child is *not aware* of sex-role
demands, and the climate created should not center
on the child's sex; if demands are made on the basis
of sex, difficulties may soon arise.

Early Childhood

Begins to identify with male and female adults in
different ways: Mommy cooks, Daddy shaves. (However, this is becoming more and more difficult in our
society; TV commercials, for example, show men
and women both shaving, wearing pants, etc.).

Late Childhood

Singles out own sex as companions; similarity of
dress, hair, toys; knowledge of physical differences
gives real evidence of development.

Recognition of Bodily Development

Infancy

Recognizes patterns of feeding, toileting, etc., and
begins to adapt.

Early Childhood

Differences in activity **due** to changes in muscular abilities. Child recognizes expectations of others and makes effort to live up to them.

Late Childhood

Awareness that differences in activities are related to sex differences. (Many activities are not based on actual physical differences but rather on what "should" be expected from "a boy" or "a girl." This may cause the child some confusion when siblings are given special privileges solely on the basis of sex.)

Growing Physical Self

Infancy

Move toward physical equilibrium: sitting, walking; move toward visual-motor coordination; eye-hand, eye-hand-mouth, hand-to-hand movements. Life rhythm is rest and activity; reliable patterns of sleep and play.

Early Childhood

Development of large-muscle control. Desire to use new control—jumping, building, climbing, dancing, throwing, painting, walking. With more security, new activities are created which combine use both of large and of small muscles—finger painting, clay work, bicycling, skating, writing.

Late Childhood

Period of great absorbency. Child has good command of his body and is now eager to push it to its limits. Begins to develop insight; he can now structure physical activities to enhance beginning skills: for example, use of small muscles in writing, sewing, building small objects.

Self as a Perceiver and Controller of the Physical World

Infancy

Continuous explorative behavior to *sense* the physical world through sight, touch, smell, taste, biting, hearing.

Early Childhood

Through adults' intervention, restrictions imposed by environment; begins to make judgments on physical states (hot, cold, light, dark) and on causality (planes go up into the sky, wheels move a car).

Late Childhood

Movement toward "logical" explanations for natural phenomena (Santa Claus lives in the mountains and makes the snow). Also, the child is now in command of his own body and is able to relate cause and effect in a rudimentary way. Thus he can, and does, make judgments affecting his own behavior.

Abilities as Inner Extensions to the Outer World

Infancy

Beginning of preverbal communication (smiles, pat-a-cake, cries, banging); develops verbal communication (uses syllables and words understood by mothering one); responds to speech of adults and others. Beginnings of nonverbal structuring in thought; for the child, physical aspects of objects define the object (for example, round ball is differentiated from cubed block).

Early Childhood

Creation and elaboration of language patterns shared with others; clearer definition of nonverbal structuring in thought; all things past are "yesterday."

Late Childhood

Utilizing language patterns to affect others; nuances in word usage. Independent choice of words tailored to the conversation. Growing ability to understand reasons; use of insight in making judgments.

Self and the World

Infancy

At this stage one *is* the world; child moves slowly toward differentiation between self and others.

Early Childhood

Begins to see differences between his world and adults' world. His own place seems a part of his physical condition—"when I grow up," etc.

Late Childhood

Begins to sort out people, and phenomena, on basis of differences. Rudiments of scientific thinking emerge; hypotheses are formed and tested; judgments are based on observation; thinking becomes qualitative.

Part II

Reciprocal Activity:
Preliminaries

Intellectual growth, as we know, requires early organization of the child's motor organs, which involves not only muscles but nerves and brain as well. We know that throughout life movement and intellectual growth are interdependent. Developmental exercises in the form of meaningful activities, therefore, should be sequential. Each child is an individual with his own tempo of growth, and the activities he is offered should follow one another according to his abilities at any given stage.

The learning process is essentially indirect; the adult's role in it is akin to that of the stage director. A good director makes himself thoroughly familiar with his materials, prepares the space, and sets the stage so that the action of the play can go forward. He guides, not dictates. Just as he lets an actor walk across the stage in his own individual way, so the mother should let her child move in *his* special way. The child is the star. The parent should be the participating audience without becoming a schoolteacher. Sometimes, however, parents

27

are rebuffed; the child wants to be left alone. On the other hand, parents themselves may feel unable, or be unwilling, to participate. When this happens, the impasse can be broken by fixing a regular daily period when parent and child can do things together—wash dishes, make beds, iron, read, sing, dance, work with peg sets, have a tea party, or perform the activities outlined later in this book.

What is important is that the child should come to understand that he can have his mother or father all to himself for a specific period each day. Even if there is more than one preschooler in the family, an unbroken stretch of time will still give each child the feeling he is getting exclusive attention. If you can work with one child while another takes a nap, all the better—for a while, at least, the child won't have to share his parent.

It is important, also, that the child be able to feel, occasionally, that for a particular period he is running the show. The child who is with his mother all day—who goes for a walk with her, sits in the cart as she does the marketing, plays in the yard or playground while she watches, helps her drive the car, runs small errands around the house for her—is most assuredly taking part in the life of the home. But all these activities have adult goals. Mothers may feel they are giving their full time to "being home" with their children when the child may actually be getting no more than a few minutes of her *focused interest*. The idea behind deliberately setting aside a specific time for a definite activity is to communicate to the child that there is time, for a very special one-to-one relationship between them.

Children want to *do*. Perhaps more important, they want to "do" well. All children have a natural drive toward self-mastery. In addition, as we have noted, they need an audience. Youngsters like to try things, to experiment, but whether they succeed or fail is sometimes of secondary importance. It is *recognition* that spurs them on toward further experiment and mastery. Self-mastery is the key to our individuality, and we begin to move toward it by using whatever abilities and experience we possess. In doing this we involve others. We need constant reaffirmation, and we get it by looking at the image of ourselves reflected by others. Awareness of this comes early in life, and a daily period of special activity is one way in which a child wins respect and recognition.

The activity session set aside each day should not come right before a nap or a visit because many children feel they want to be physically close to their mothers and aren't quite ready for activity. The best time will depend on the child's schedule, and on how well you fit the activity into the rhythm of his day. As for the place you choose, this will depend largely on the activity. But whether it is the floor or a table, the area should be cleared of everything except the materials to be used. Chairs should be of a size suitable for the child. If daylight is the primary source of light, the child should be seated so that he is not facing it directly. The room temperature should be comfortable; on the cool side, if anything, for children tend to be sluggish or touchy in overheated rooms.

Before introducing an activity to the child, do it yourself several times, step by step, so that you are thoroughly familiar with the procedure and understand the possibilities. As you read the individual explanations, the underlying rationale of each activity should emerge.

Each activity or "lesson," is divided into two parts: Introduction and action.

Introduction

Here are four important guidelines:

1. Enthusiasm for the interpersonal situation and for the activity itself must be felt by the adult and conveyed to the child if full benefit from the activity is to be realized. An atmosphere of liveliness and anticipation is most important. Children respond to it and are attracted by it.

2. The real role of the adult here is to present the material and activity in such a way as to make it possible for the child to have some initial success. (Note: These activities can be "misused." If, for example, the parent misjudges the degree of interest the child has and insists on pushing along with the activity when the child is clearly not ready for it, he may balk later on. Your enthusiasm must be leavened with an objective evaluation of what the child has been doing and what he appears to be ready for. This is the most critical aspect of the reciprocal relationship, for if the timing is wrong, the situation is likely to thrust you into the teacher's role. When the timing is right, your child's spontaneity and pleasure blend with your own enthusiasm into the mixture of warmth and affection that good parent-child relationships are made of.)

3. If your child has difficulty with the material, observe him for a while before doing anything about it. Many difficulties are self-correcting; as the activity progresses, the child often sees his mistakes and makes the appropriate changes. This is perhaps one of the most important features of "constructive" activity, because it is the child himself who recognizes the need for a different approach and who attempts to solve the problem. If your child's interest begins to wander, however, and he takes to sticking pegs into the food in the refrigerator or something equally unrelated to the business at hand, then it's a good time to stop.

4. The child should experience what is called a "good finish." This means that when he is finished with an activity he should be obliged to pick up the pieces and return materials to their proper place. You can make it easier for him by providing boxes, bags, or shelves, and by establishing a fixed place for keeping the materials. This type of "filing" is respected by the child, and it encourages him to see and choose the activities in a meaningful way. Digging into a disorganized play-box promotes disorderly habits. Also, by having the material in a fixed, accessible place, the child is permitted the right of choice without the thwarting and often destructive effects of having to rummage around.

    The methods outlined here are meant as a working guide which, we hope, will enable you to present the activities in a way to make the child want to participate. You should bear in mind, also, that generally the child will not only participate, but also will create new ways of treating the material. By all means, encourage him.

Action

Since this part of the activity involves more language than the first, beware. Depending on the age and maturity of the child, the amount of descriptive language you use should be kept to the minimum; you will be the best judge of that. The reason for it is simple. The child will get more benefit from an activity if he is encouraged to make his own observations, and if he comes to understand the various differences in dimensions, qualities, etc. which he experiences, than if he has it all handed to him on a platter. Remember to speak softly and in a way to intrigue the child. Pronounce your words correctly and clearly, so that the various sound components are blended into a correct yet ordinary speech pattern. Avoid exaggeration.

There are three stages to this part of the activity:

1. The association of names with sensory experiences. Name the item clearly: "This is the peg," "This is the elastic length," etc. It is important to use the correct names and to omit superfluous or nonspecific descriptive words. The child should be able to feel he is being given reliable information. Later, through play, he can attach

his own descriptive adjectives and adverbs to names and activities.

2. The child's interest in, and capacity for, relating names to objects and acts should be verified. The parent does this by allowing the child some time to work or handle the material, and then saying: "Point to the peg," "Point to the elastic length," etc. The child may respond by pointing to the correct item or by naming and touching it. This should be done several times during the next few minutes to make sure the child really understands (if acts and names are well entrenched in the child's vocabulary, a single query is quite sufficient; don't tell him what he already knows as if it were new information). When a child does not retain the names, then question him from time to time so that he will not feel threatened by his own attempts to respond.

3. In this stage, you determine whether the child can verbally identify the material. As you hold up the peg or elastic, ask him, "What is this?"

For the parent, the most interesting part of these activities is the possibility of developing one's own approach to the child's language needs. The three-stage "lesson" is merely a basic outline meant to be "filled in" by each parent to suit the language development of his children. You can tap the richness of the language by having the child describe things (the elastic is "stretchy," "bouncy"; it "moves" or it "pinches," etc.) and then discussing his reactions. Imagination, exploration, and inventiveness with words, especially descriptives such as adverbs and adjectives, should be encouraged. Children may have large vocabularies (learned, in many instances, from TV commercials), but unless they have the opportunity for real conversation, using "real" words, they are going to speak—and think—in very shallow terms.

Visual Discrimination:
Fine Muscle Coordination:
Form — Lines

Materials

An 18-inch square of red, dark blue, or green felt, or several 9-inch squares of felt in several vivid colors. (Many yard-goods stores sell these squares)

A box of regular-sized toothpicks

Setup

Floor or table space
Felt cloth folded in half
Mat and box of toothpicks

Approach and Activity

There are many packaged games that are larger and more colorful, but this activity has the great advantage of requiring very little space; it can be slipped into a handbag, which makes it an ideal take-along on trips. It serves as a sickbed activity or as a party game (with several 9-inch squares and children either working on their own or on a group project).

One purpose of the activity is to discipline eye-hand movements. Children are accustomed to complicated hand and eye movements, as, for example, in watching TV or in washing themselves. Yet few activities have the interest power of block building or bicycle riding and also afford such excellent use of both eye and hand.

1. Unfold the cloth. (Simple—but it is a good idea to have the child become aware of folding the cloth because it is an additional hand exercise and also because, when the work is completed,

the cloth will be folded again to be put away until next time.)

2. Place the box of toothpicks above the cloth, either toward the right or the left corner, depending on handedness of the child (right-handed, right corner).

3. Take several toothpicks from the box and hold one of them between thumb and index finger of left hand. Run index finger of right hand up and down surface.

4. As you do this, let the child pick up a toothpick and ask him to feel it. Talk about what you both feel; smoothness, points, thinness, thickness, etc.

5. After this exploratory period, suggest that, since the toothpicks are somewhat like straight lines, it is possible to make pictures from them. If the child hesitates, direct his attention to the door, window, or floor. But, if at all possible, let him start to arrange the toothpicks in some pattern.

6. Games can be made if: (a) you suggest an object he can make; (b) he makes an object and you guess what it is; (c) you invent a two-man game like dominoes, each taking turns creating an unknown.

7. Once the child seems pleased with the activity, encourage him to do whatever he can with 8 sticks, say, then 10 sticks, and so on. In fact, try to lead him to create any figure he can, since the

main objective is to manipulate the material using both hand and eye.

Some Implications

Children need opportunities to create things that serve no other purpose than to be created. We place so much emotional emphasis on so many things, that it is not easy for children to find as much value in the doing as in the final product. Yet, this is the very element in all education—and in life itself for that matter—that is so basic to richness of thought and spirit. The ability to create "things that never were or could be," as well as more familiar configurations, gives pleasure and meaning to the child.

At the same time, he is able to exercise and coordinate hand and eye, two disparate parts of the body. The pleasure and meaning that the initial thrust of the infant's hand into his mouth gives him can often be observed by a parent. We see a positioning of the fist in space, the eye focusing upon it; the intense movement toward the face; and, finally, successful contact with the mouth. According to William James, a true sense of self begins when the infant's eye first guides his hand to his mouth. There can be little doubt that the child's sense of self and his mastery of his world is greatly enhanced by his continuing discovery of himself as a creator.

Visual Discrimination: Form—Lines

Materials

Pegboard—minimum width, 12 inches; maximum
width, 36 inches; minimum length, 24 inches;
maximum length, 48 inches

Mounting screws and backers, in kit form

Elastic—flat, ¼ inch, in black and white; round, in
black and white. Amount depends on size of
board; it's good to have equal amounts of each
shape and color; approximately 3 yards of each
should be adequate

Golf tees and/or colored pegs, 24 in all

Setup

1. Paint the pegboard with a lacquer-like paint
    such as Lacaloid, in any one of these colors:
    bright yellow, vivid pink, bright light blue or
    white.

2. When the board is thoroughly dry and the
    surface appears smooth and shiny (this may
    require 2 coats of paint), string the elastic. This
    stringing depends on the size of the board.
    However, it is important to establish a pattern
    (which need not be symmetrical). Assuming that
    the piece is 24 inches by 48 inches, the stringing
    might go like this:

    a. Using the 24-inch dimension as width and
       the 48-inch dimension as length, take the
       widest piece of black elastic and run it 2
       inches through to the back, in a hole 2 inches
       from both top and side; double-knot in back.
    b. Run the piece straight down on the front

surface to hole 2 inches in from both bottom
and side and push through hole to the back.

c. Skip 5 holes, enter sixth from the back.
Bring elastic through to the front and carry
straight up to the top line (2 inches from
top), run through to the back and double
knot, leaving a 2-inch tail. Pull elastic so that
each front strip is tight.

d. Take round white elastic and begin at second
hole from first strip of black. Run to back
and fasten to black end by knotting.

e. Run piece straight down to second hole from
bottom; push from front to back, bring out
in second hole over, and run strip straight up,
bringing it out to the back. Take some piece
along back to sixth hole away and bring to
front through hole, run straight down, pull-
ing all 3 verticals taut; knot several times,
leaving a 4-inch piece to be knotted later.

f. Turn board around so that the side on the
left will now be on the right and repeat
design, substituting wide white elastic for the
wide black, and round black for the round
white. It is important that all verticals be
taut and all ends securely tied, preferably to
each other.

3. Using standard pegboard mounting kit (cost
about 39 cents), mount the board on a door or
wall (doors are better since they are rarely used
for other purposes). Position the board so that
at least two-thirds of the surface is within arm's
reach of the child.

4. Place pegs and tees along left and right side holes in a vertical pattern. The first row of holes is a good holding place since it is outside the patternwork area.

Approach and Activity

Since the board is the focal point, little preparation is needed for the child. However, as with most activities, it is wise to show the child how to use the material before leaving him to his own pleasure. The reason for this is quite simple. Young children are limited in their physical skills. These activities are designed to help develop such skills, and so it is important that the child be shown what the materials are and how to handle them.

This does not mean that you are showing the child how to "be creative"; nor are you presenting him with a model and taking his freedom away from him. On the contrary, the child, armed with the materials and the means to use them, will then have the real sense of freedom needed to create.

The procedure may follow this pattern:

1. A little conversation on "lines," perhaps pointing out lamp cords, or lines in the outline of a room, a rug, or piece of furniture.

2. Go over the board and mention the fact that the lines on the board can be stretched and moved about.

3. Finger a midpoint of elastic, pull it carefully toward you and let it snap back.

4. Take a peg from the side and let the child touch it to feel its length, width, roundness. Take the peg back into your hand.

5. Have the child run his fingers over the peg board so that he can touch the smooth part, the holes, the stretchy elastics. Use this time for some conversation, mentioning these descriptive words.

6. Take the peg and place it in a hole at random.

7. Then take any length of elastic and stretch it toward the peg.

8. Go from left to right over the peg with the elastic if you come from the left side; from right to left if you come from the right side, so that the length now has three fixed points rather than the original two.

9. Let the child do steps 6, 7, and 8. Give him an opportunity to talk, if this seems timely.

10. Then sit by while he works on his design.

It is important that the child not be made to feel he has to stay with the activity for a prescribed length of time, or that he has to do it all. Once the original presentation is made the board becomes a vehicle for his pleasure. (Perhaps you can manage a few movements of your own when he is not looking; this is quite addicting.)

Some Implications

This activity board serves the child in several unique ways: It affords him the opportunity to work at something which does not have definite end; there is always the chance for continued change and more activity. There are no standards in the sense of any "proper" way of handling the materials. "Success" depends solely on the child's pleasure in using the materials and seeing what he can do with them. This is an important factor in child's play since it can help free him to work on creative activities and relationships without the burden of producing "a thing."

Manipulation of the material involves finger, hand, and arm movements, and benefits from the exercise are cumulative. As the child works, he trains his eye-hand movements while exercising his visual and aesthetic discrimination. He is constantly "judging" his work and actions and can reshape them to experiment or just to please himself.

The value to the child of such an activity lies in his ability to exploit the material; to shape it to his own design, a design which emerges through manipulation of the material rather than through a predetermined pattern. In a sense, the child is being permitted to develop physical skills of manipulation and coordination while engaging in creative construction of something. While the value of creative arts as such cannot be stressed enough, it is not uncommon for children to engage in them without realizing the sense of mastery they achieve, over both their body and reality, a mastery so important to their total development.

Visual Discrimination:
Form—Shapes

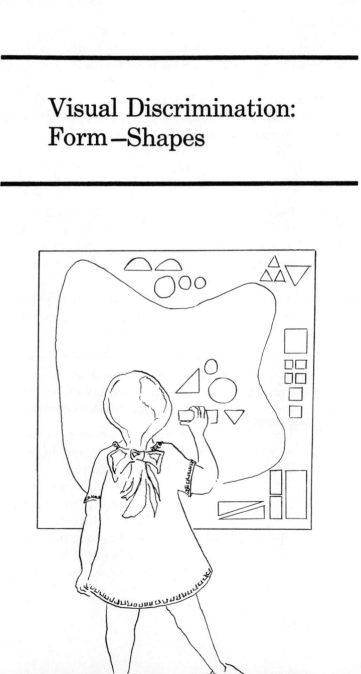

Materials

Pegboard, 2 feet by 2 feet

Mounting screws and backers for pegboard, in kit
form

Pegs, approximately 2 dozen

Plastic household sponges, 12 2-inch by 4-inch pieces
in pastel shades

Sobo glue

Setup

1. Paint the pegboard white in a lacquer-like paint
    such as Lacaloid. If you wish, a free-form
    pattern can be painted—in a pastel color, giving
    the illusion of an irregular 3-inch border to be
    created. This border may act as a limit for work
    space, as an added dimension of manipulation,
    and as a divider for storing unused pieces from
    the composition being made.

2. When the board is thoroughly dry, use the
    standard kit to mount it on a closet door or on
    free wall space, making sure the midsection of
    the board is just above the child's eye level.

3. The following patterns can be used to cut out
    geometric shapes from the sponge rectangles:

Circles (Pink)	1—3-inch diameter
	1—3-inch diameter, cut in two along the diameter
	2—1½-inch diameter
Squares (Blue)	1—3 inches by 3 inches
	2—2 inches by 2 inches
	4—1½ inches by 1½ inches

Rectangles (Green) 1—3 inches by 5 inches

2—2½ inches by 3 inches

2—triangles made by a diagonal cut on another 3-inch by 5-inch rectangle

Triangles (Yellow) 3 triangles made by using 5-inch base, cutting diagonally up to opposite upper edge midpoint from both lower edges.

3 triangles made by using 3-inch base, cutting diagonally upward to opposite upper edge midpoint from both lower sides.

4 triangles made by making one 3 inch square, then cutting this diagonally. Cut remainder (2-inch by 3-inch piece) diagonally so that you have two large triangles and two smaller right triangles.

4. Fasten each cut piece to a peg in the following manner:

a. At tip of peg, smooth some Sobo glue around upper ½ inch.

b. At the center of cut sponge piece, insert the peg end with Sobo on it. Hold it in place until the peg is firm. Try not to let the peg show through the right side surface of sponge.

   c. Set the sponge on a flat surface so that the peg projects upward to dry.

   d. Repeat a, b, and c for all pieces.

   e. If the space on the sponge seems too large, place a soft tissue dipped in Sobo glue into it.

Approach and Activity

This form board is similar to the line-form board in that it affords the child a motor activity related to visual manipulation of objects. Since it is large and colorful, the child will be easily attracted to it. Also the individual objects are in geometric shape, making the board even more interesting when it is first presented to him. Adult and child can be seated on the floor for the first session.

1. The forms can be arranged in each of the four corners of the board, according to shape (and therefore color as well).

2. The child should be given a round form first, since this is an unbroken line and the easiest shape for him to understand. Remove the shape from the board by placing your thumb on the outside surface, at the point above the peg. Move your index and middle fingers so that the peg is positioned between them and raise your hand from the board. In this way the peg is supported as it is removed from the board and the sponge is moved toward the peg rather than away from it. This position of the fingers is similar to that used in holding a writing tool.

3. Have the child run his second and third fingers around the outer surface of the form. Let him do this as many times as he likes.

4. Repeat this with the rectangle, square, and triangle, in that order. Take care not to fatigue the child. If he seems restless then stop at two shapes and proceed to 5.

5. Place several sponge shapes on the board, handling each piece in the proper way, so that some grouping emerges.

6. Suggest to the child that he can use some or all of these shapes to make something that will "surprise" him. Encourage him to move the shapes about as he will. No direction should be given to place any particular shape next to another, and the names of the shapes should not be used at this early stage. After several weeks or months, the child himself will relate the shapes to other shapes in his environment and will name them. At this point, a session involving the proper names of the four shapes can be pleasurable.

Some Implications

The relevance of shape both to reading and to writing is of great importance, since both rely heavily on a tactile muscular sense as well as a visual sense. Dr. Montessori found that the child's association of the tactile muscular sense with the visual helps to a marked degree in the perception of shapes. The softness of the sponge encour-

ages the child to feel it, an action which, while physically
pleasurable, is also a stimulus. Differences among the
shapes will be experienced through touch and sight and
will thus lead to qualitative comparison and judgment.

The forming of unique "pictures" adds to the
continuing interest this activity has for the child. The
possibility of creating many different compositions is a
spur to further activity. As a prereading and prewriting
activity, it affords the child experience with changed
shapes and with compositions derived from various
shapes. It is a kind of prelude to the stage in which he
begins to form letters themselves. Although most letters
in manuscript form are made with straight lines and some
curves, the shift to a cursive-writing letter is sometimes
very difficult for the child. This activity gives him early
experience with line and shape and in manipulation of
these elements with fingers and hand. At an early age,
basic learnings are possible which can ease later learning
that reveals elements of sameness to the experienced
child.

Visual Discrimination: Form

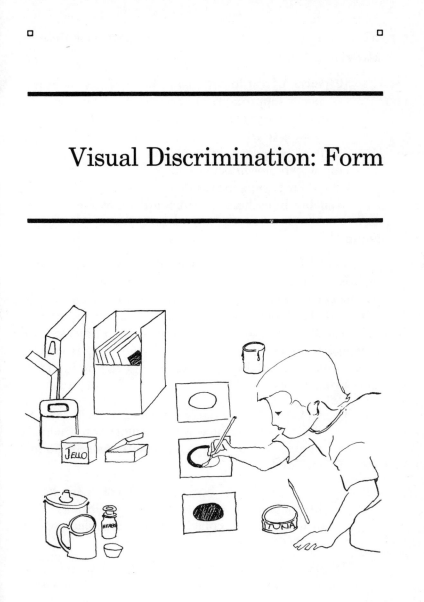

Materials

> 30 pieces of cardboard from men's shirts or heavy
>   paper—approximately 8 inches by 10 inches
> 1 large, empty cereal box, large enough for card-
>   boards to fit
> Bottle of tempera paint (red, green, or blue)
> Thin watercolor brush
> 1-inch tempera paintbrush
> Available household or cupboard items (see Setup)

Setup

Since this activity involves the contents of cup-
boards, refrigerators, or closets, an initial search by the
parent is necessary in order to attempt to find: 5 objects
with circular bases, each of a different size (spice jar,
baby food jar, cans of different sizes, etc.); 5 objects with
rectangular bases of various sizes (Jell-o box, rice box,
cereal box, etc.). Make sure these things can be found in
their usual places.

1. Cut the empty large cereal box as shown in
   illustration so box will resemble some napkin
   boxes, with a third of one side and all of the top
   cut away.

2. Paint outside of box with tempera, using larger
   brush (a child can easily do the painting). This
   will be the receptacle for the complete set of
   cards.

3. Take each of your 10 objects and in pencil trace
   the outline of each base on each of 3 separate
   pieces of cardboard—a total of 30—cards.

4. Make 3 groups of these cards, 10 different shapes in each group.

5. *Group 1:* With the watercolor brush and the tempera paint (or with magic markers), go over the outline in as thin a line as possible.
   Group 2: With the larger brush, paint as heavy a line as possible using the penciled outline as the outermost edge.
   Group 3: With the larger brush, paint in the whole figure, again being careful to use the penciled line as the outermost edge.

6. When all the cards are dry, place them in group order in the newly made receptacle.

Approach and Activity

This activity has many possibilities. It can be hide-and-seek, a partner game, a group game or a one-man game of one-upmanship. The important thing is that the child is attempting to relate visual image and substance. This is rudimentary geometry, since we begin with the solidly colored cards and move to the more abstract thin-edged configurations. Another aspect of great interest to the child is his own explorations. He sees three-dimensioned objects in relation to two-dimensional forms. While this may seem a difficult learning for the adult, the child manipulates, observes, and questions (to himself and aloud) in such a way that germinative conceptualization takes place.

There are several possible introductions to this activity as well as many possible improvisations that may follow. The work area can be either on the floor or on a tabletop. Since the cards are quite large, the larger the space the better. If you use the floor, a small rug (a remnant or area rug) can serve as an "island" on which the child can place some of the materials and possibly himself.

A.   1.   Set aside on the rug several of the cans and boxes as well as the box containing the cards.

2.   Sit down with the child and have a short conversation about touching things (things he likes to touch, their textures, shapes, etc.).

3.   Take out the *solidly* painted cards with the circles on them. Mix them up and place them down at random in front of the child. Ask him to find the largest one, then the smallest. Have him place the largest at the extreme right and the smallest at the far left. Now let him find the next largest, and so on until he has arranged the entire set from left to right in order of size.

4.   Ask the child to take the cans and jars set aside on the rug and see if he can match them with the painted spaces on the cards. You might begin by asking him to find the card with the smallest figure. Let him continue on his own until he completes the series of five. He should be able to see his errors as he makes them; if he doesn't, he will when he completes the series.

5. After the child has enjoyed doing 4, continue with the rectangular objects in the same way. At this point the child will enjoy running his fingers around the sides of the round and rectangular objects to feel the roundness (no corners) and the "rectangularness" (4 corners, 2 short sides, 2 longer sides).

B. 1. Another time, you may lay out the cards as in A-1 and then ask the child to continue by laying out the heavily outlined cards in corresponding order beneath. Finally, let him lay out the thinly outlined cards in matching order. This can be done in two ways:

2. He can then match objects and figure by using any of the three groups. You could also sometime supply three of each—that is, three identical soup cans, three jars, etc., so that all the spaces are filled.

3. This activity can be like a game for several children, with each one taking a turn. Or it can be set up with 9 cards and played like tic-tac-toe.

4. It can be a hide-and-seek game, with the child being shown a card and asked to go to the closet to find the matching object.

Some Implications

Visual recognition of shape and size is an important factor in later learning related not only to reading, but also to arithmetic. Letters are constructed and perceived by relating shape to shape, size to size, and size to shape. All letters are relationships between shape and shape and between size and shape. The same holds for numbers.

Basic to such discrimination is early experience with shapes and sizes, so that the child can actually see the differences between large and small, for example, or between circle and rectangle. The number of objects chosen can be expanded to include other shapes such as ovals, triangles, squares, trapezoids, etc., depending on what you find around the house. In this age of plastic packaging, you'll be amazed at the interesting shapes you can find formed by the bottom, top, or side of a container of detergent!

The child engages in this activity on his own once the initial encounter is made. However, since two can also play, the parent can always "sit awhile" and "be with" his child on an intellectual level. Looking at geometric shapes helps the child understand both his man-made and his natural environments.

Visual Discrimination:
Form II

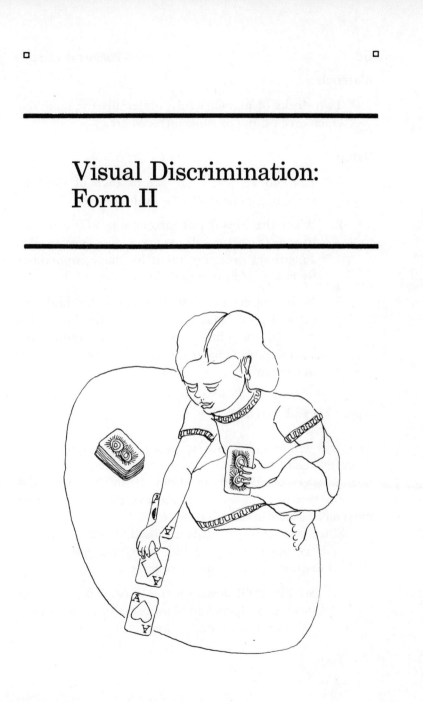

Materials

> Two decks of playing cards, preferably the same size
> Open area on rug or solid-surfaced area

Setup

1. Lay out vertically the ace of each of the four suits, using one deck as a beginning activity.

2. When the idea is put into action, you can then use as many cards as you like up to 52, sometimes grouping them by shape, sometimes by color, and sometimes by number.

3. It is important that the cards be laid out vertically, so that matching can be done horizontally. Reading vision depends upon horizontal movement of the eyes rather than vertical movement.

Approach and Activity

This is a rather quiet activity that is especially effective when the child has just awakened from a nap or rest and does not yet want to move about. It involves hand and eye movements. The eye is being exercised in left-right movement as the matching is done.

Since two decks of cards are used, it is important to have a large open area available, such as a floor or rug clear of distracting or inhibiting objects.

1. Sit the child down on the floor. Take off your shoes or slippers and place them in front of you. Ask the child to do likewise.

2. Take one of your shoes and put ıι midway between you and the child. Ask him to find the one that is the same (like) (match) (similar) as the one placed in the open area. If he makes the right choice, compliment him by clapping or exclaiming. If he does not, place the two shoes next to each other, showing him that one is larger or smaller than the other. For a true match they must be the same shape, length, width, color.

3. You can also match feet and hands to see differences.

4. Place the shoes to one side or put them on.

5. Now take both decks of cards and place them in front of you. (Preshuffle them into order for this first attempt.)

6. Select the joker, ace of diamonds and ace of hearts. Place them vertically with about an inch of space between. Take the deck from which you have removed the cards and put it to your left.

7. Place the second deck flat on the group in front of the child. Take the top card and see if it matches any of the three on the rug. If it does not, begin making a pile by placing it face down a few inches from the drawing deck. Take the next card and look at it (perhaps you will have placed a matching one here). If it matches, place it next to its twin. Let the child continue until all three are matched. It is important that the

cards be handled in an orderly way and that the
first encounter be leisurely.

8. When the three cards are matched, you may lay
down more cards from your original deck and
let the child begin the matching. Taking turns
might be pleasant. This activity, done at different times, can eventually begin with all 52 cards.

Some Implications

This activity can be done anywhere—sickbed, train, car,
beach, place, park, the child's own room. Sometimes
after particularly rousing activity or after a meal, the
child cannot unwind. This is an activity that is lively
enough for the child yet does not stimulate random
motor behavior. The action is visual and mental.

What the child is doing is matching visual form to
visual form. This is a kind of sight recognition that is part
of "reading readiness" programs. As you see, the recognition of symbols and shapes really leads to matching, and
successful matching is an important victory for preschool
children. Bombarded by innumerable visual stimuli—in
the market, on television, in the home—the child makes a
definite effort to relate similar objects to each other. The
product he sees on TV, then later "live," on the market
counter or kitchen shelf, delights the child. This delight
has little to do with physical possession; rather, he is
delighted by his awareness that he can "substantiate" the
product by finding something like it at home.

The pleasure children take in matching is much like
the pleasure they find in a new sound that can be
repeated and related endlessly.

The physical aspects of this activity help foster a sense of order and orderliness which are enjoyed by the preschooler.

Visual Discrimination: Dimensions

Materials

Shelf of books

Setup

Remove the books from the shelf and place them in a clear area with no traffic, not too far from the emptied shelf.

Approach and Activity

This activity has two preconditions: that the child be able to handle books carefully and that the bookshelves be sturdy. The activity involves three aspects of dimension—height, width, and volume. It is suggested that the parent select *one* aspect at a time; the procedure is much the same for each.

For example:

1. Walk over to a full-length mirror and stand side by side with your child. Ask him if he can see which of you is shorter, which of you is taller. Do the same with things like lamps and tables, doors and chests, windows and drapes, etc.

2. Take two books of different sizes from the group. Ask the child to show you the taller one (spine perpendicular to floor), then the shorter one.

3. Suggest that he place all the books back on the shelf in descending or ascending order of size.

Some Implications

To strengthen our perception of dimension it is necessary to use our perceptions in meaningful ways. In fact, the possibility of creating new relationships and structures rests upon the ability to manipulate our environment in such a way as to make new forms from old. How can a child perceive symmetry in nature and in his man-made environment unless he has an understanding of line, height, width?

This activity is multileveled. The eye as perceiver, the hand as perceiver and manipulator, the arm as manipulator, and the body as vehicle for gross manipulatory action are all called into play.

The activity also has side benefits for Mother. By selecting a different shelf each time, she can get it washed and dusted while it is empty. The books can be dusted by the child. Cleaning bookshelves is boring and tiresome, but if it is part of a larger activity it becomes effortless.

Visual Discrimination: Dimensions II

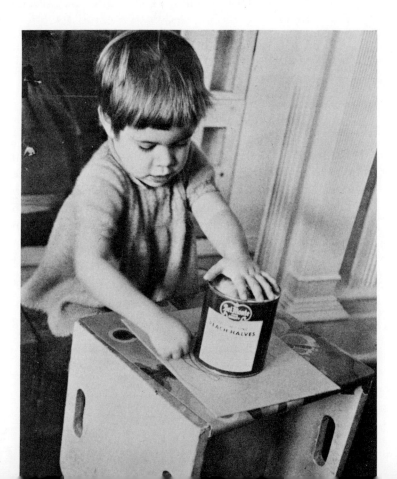

Materials

Several cardboards from Father's shirts
Red crayon
A shelf of canned goods in a closet

Setup

1. Take a wide selection of cans generally found in the food closet and place them all on a low shelf or on a large tray.

2. Set a can down on a cardboard and, with the red crayon, draw around its circumference several times.

3. Do this with other cans of various sizes on at least three cards, drawing three or more configurations.

Approach and Activity

This should be both a visual activity and a gross physical one. It is ideal for times when Mother must be in the kitchen and the child wants to "help." The parent may point out one or another figure and ask the child to search for it in a closet at some distance. However, for an introduction the following procedure seems most feasible.

1. Bring the cards into the kitchen and spread them out on the table or floor in an area where the child can move about freely without getting into your way.

2. Tell him that each circle can be filled by a specific can from a specific shelf in the closet. Show him *that* shelf.

3. Let him take a can and try to find the space that it will fill on the cards.

4. If he cannot find the space, let him put the can down where he is working.

5. Let him continue with other cans until he fills all the other spaces. This activity has a built-in corrector. If one can is placed on a space too large for it, the child can actually see the mistake. He will end up with another can in a space too small. Thus if multiple errors are made, visual clues to the mismatching, will be evident.

Some Implications

One's home has a supermarket quality about it, especially food closets. Manufacturers size and color their products in very individual ways. Children who are frequently taken to the market become familiar with brand names and identifications. Like much else in the world, these objects can mean many things and could be used in various ways. The kitchen and pantry have great attraction for children. Even if the most wonderful miniature carousel were set up in their own room, for example, children would still be drawn to the kitchen. It is a place of action, mystery, and magic. Here, many an infant has his first manipulative experiences and his first experiences with sound and/or with visual-size discrimination.

This activity is designed to develop the child's ability to discern and isolate one dimension (width) in a three-dimensioned object. This is quite a sophisticated process, brought to the child's level of interest and manipulatory possibilities by the choice of the material used. The fingers, the hands, and the arm are all used during this activity. Interesting relationships may also appear; for example, how can the same circle accommodate both a short can and a tall can?

Visual Discrimination:
Dimension—Length

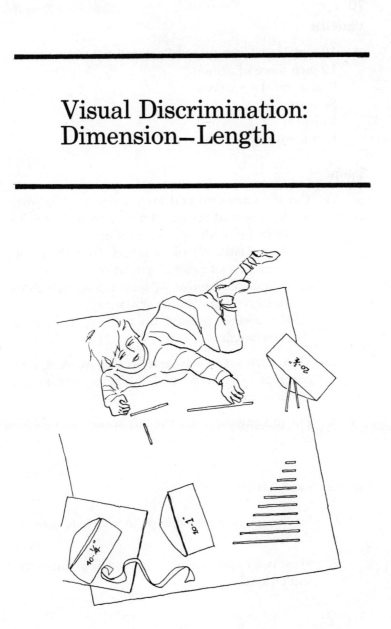

Materials

12-inch by 12-inch piece of colored felt
12-inch piece of ribbon
Box of drinking straws
Scissors
Ruler
Letter envelopes

Setup

1. Cut the straws into different lengths, as follows:
    a. A graduated set of 10 pieces from 1 inch to 10 inches with 1-inch gradations.
    b. A graduated set of 20 pieces, from ½ inch to 10 inches with ½-inch gradations.
    c. A graduated set of 40 pieces, from ¼ inch to 10 inches with ¼-inch gradations.
        If straws are colored, use a different color for each length.

2. Place each set in a separate envelope. Mark each envelope with a symbol the same size as the smallest piece.

3. Put the envelopes on the left square and fold it over; tie it with the ribbon.

Approach and Activity

1. Sit at a good-sized table or in a cleared area on the floor.

2. Place roll of felt before child and have him untie and unfold it.

3. Take the 1-inch envelope and set it on mat. Place the other two envelopes to the side.

4. Have the child shake up the envelope and spill out the contents on the mat.

5. Ask him to try to find the largest piece, then the smallest piece. Let him place them toward either side of the mat.

6. Now ask him to arrange the other pieces in order of size between these two extremes. (He may want to arrange them with spaces between or close together.)

7. If he is interested, continue with ½-inch pieces and then ¼-inch pieces.

8. Once the child has done all three lengths he may want to mix up the sets. If he does, he will find interesting possibilities, and, we hope, he will ask you some interesting questions.

9. The child should be encouraged to place a set of lengths into each envelope when he completes the task.

Some Implications

One-inch differences are easily handled by both eye and hand, but ½-inch differences are somewhat more difficult, and ¼-inch differences are quite challenging and difficult for the child. This is the kind of activity that lends itself to the child's pleasure. After he has repeated the exercise, he will begin to experiment with relationships and use the lengths to construct figures and possibly pictures. Since the fingers have to be used to pick up each piece, the child is able to exercise the small muscles in his hand.

This is a good open-end activity that also gives the child material for visualization.

Visual Discrimination:
Spatial Relationships

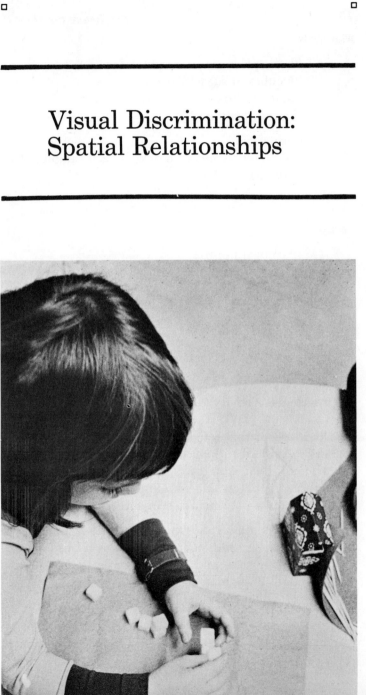

Materials

> A. Plastic place-mat in bright color
> 25 cubes of sugar (Dots)
> Band-Aid box covered with Contact
> ½ yard of ribbon
>
> B. Carpet mat
> Children's wooden blocks (for example, Play-
> skool)

Setup

> 1. Put sugar in box.
>
> 2. Cover box with Contact.
>
> 3. Place box in mat and fold mat over.
>
> 4. Tie with ribbon.

Approach and Activity

The purpose of this activity is to provide the child with
exercises designed to help develop pattern vision; that is,
to see and then duplicate objects arranged in space.
Therefore, the patterning should proceed from simple to
more complex arrangements, sequentially.

> 1. Since this can either be a floor or a table
> activity, find a free area and place the mat
> before the child. Let him untie the ribbon and
> unfold the mat.

2. Take out a cube of sugar and place it on the mat. Ask the child to tell you what he sees.

3. Now let him touch it and pick it up. Ask him to describe what he feels.

4. Ask him if he would like to eat it; let him describe what he tastes. (If blocks are used—forget about taste!)

5. Take two more pieces from the box and tell him that while this sugar is usually used as a food or sweetener you will be using it as building material.

6. Put a piece in the center of the mat, using thumb and index finger to pick it up. Ask the child to pick up the other piece of sugar and to place it *in front of your* piece.

7. Reset your piece. Ask him to place his piece *behind* yours.

8. Reset your piece. Ask him to place his piece *next* to yours.

9. Reset your piece. Ask him to place his piece *on top of* yours.

10. Reset your piece. Ask him to place his piece *under* yours.

11. If the child is content to go on, then proceed; to set these up, construct *one at a time,* leaving your structure up in front of him as a model.

Use your own judgment as to
the child's fatigue time.

a.

b.

.c.

d.

e.

f.

g.

h.

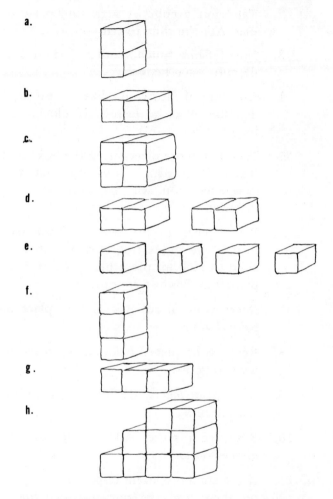

12. Once the child has gone through as many figures as he seems happy doing, suggest that he set up figures for you to duplicate.

13. When the activity time is over, let him return the cubes to the box and fold the plastic mat over it, tying it with the ribbon.

Some Implications

Children are active viewers, they can "find" Spry or Dove in the market because of their ability to retain repeated TV images. We accept children as seasoned viewers, yet we tend to see their ability "to see" as a natural, rather than as an acquired, development skill. When the child begins formal reading, he is expected to be able to see configurations (letters) in relationship to one another. When he paints, sculpts, writes, he must also *order* what he sees. Simple concepts such as *in front of, behind, above, below* are so much a part of our own daily speech that we do not pay any special attention to the child's comprehension and functional understanding of such terms. This perception of spatial relationships is a most exacting intellectual operation for the child. Activities which focus on perception of discrete parts and structuring them into wholes can greatly help the child in his understanding of such phenomena.

Both finger and eye movements are strengthened in such activity. When thumb and first digit are used to pick up the cubes, the fingers duplicate a movement used in holding a writing tool. The eye is the key to the integration of each piece toward one whole. Thus, a patterning of vision is made possible. The child will be calling on visual memory, visualization, and eye-hand coordination in carrying out the tasks.

Size and Weight

Materials

>   9-inch by 9-inch square of bright-colored felt
>   12-inch length of colored ribbon
>   Small attractive box (for example, a Band-Aid box
>   covered with Contact or felt)
>   Coins—2 half-dollars
>   2 quarters
>   2 dimes
>   2 nickels
>   Blindfold

Setup

1. Cover box with covering (if felt is used, Sobo onto container).

2. Place all coins in box.

3. Put box and blindfold on felt square, and roll into package, with contrasting piece of ribbon tie.

Approach and Activity

Coins are an important part of the environment for the preschooler. They have an interest in manipulating and identifying the different pieces. This activity is based on the Deweyan principle of using the child's environment as the means of his education. While objects of various sizes and shapes could be made or even bought, real coins are of far greater interest to the child.

This is a two-part activity in that it is fun to do both with eyes open and eyes covered.

1. After sitting down at a table or on the floor with the child, set the roll of felt before him.

2. Ask him to untie the ribbon and put it to one side.

3. Take the coin container and shake it up vigorously. Then spill out the contents on the felt mat.

4. Ask the child to match coins of the same size until all coins are paired. Set them up horizontally or vertically, but let the arrangement be of the child's design. Do not graduate the sizes.

5. Ask him to find the smallest pair; the largest pair.

6. Have him check (by manipulation) to see if the two smallest coins are exactly the same size; the two largest; the rest of the coins.

7. Put one set of coins aside.

8. Ask him to put the remaining coins in a row, from smallest to largest. (Vary this from largest to smallest at another time.)

9. Now let him match the coins set aside with the graduated set.

10. When the activity is over have the child reroll the material and help him tie it.

Some Implications

Visual constancy is an important element of both sight and intellect. It is most important that a child be able to discern an object as: (1) being different from other objects (perceive contrasts); (2) having some unique and identifying quality (establishing identities); (3) being separated from other things in his field of view (figure-ground perception).

While all of the skills learned in the early grades are based on such prior learning, little is done to understand the child's growth development in such basic abilities. One of the evidences for such growth can be seen in the paintings and drawings of children, for here they are able to manifest their ability to perceive just such data.

There is a secondary gain in this activity, derived from children's immediate enthusiasm for coins. It has long been the feeling of many teachers that if children could use real coins in classroom mathematics their enthusiasm would carry them through whatever difficulties they may have in grasping concepts. Even as early as the second and third grades, children have been able to understand both the decimal system and fractions well enough to discard the coins and work with their symbolic representations.

Visual Discrimination: Fine Motor Coordination

Materials

Assorted household objects: caps, jar and can covers, spoons, forks, boxes, plastic cups, soap boxes, empty spools of thread

Assortment of colored pencils

5-inch by 5-inch drawing paper—a good supply. (Or 6-inch by 9-inch pad of drawing paper, or 9-inch by 12-inch art paper halved on its 12-inch side and cut into 9-inch by 6-inch pieces)

Decorative box to hold cards (candy box, cookie box etc.)

A "saving can," made of a 2-pound empty coffee tin, with plastic cover

Table or desk top and child-sized chair

Setup

1. Cut the paper to uniform size and place it in the decorative box with two loose rubber bands.

2. Make a "saving can" by taking the 2-pound coffee tin and wrapping a piece of decorative paper around it and taping.

3. Find objects smaller than the paper so that their outlines can be drawn on it. Place the objects in the "saving can."

Approach and Activity

Since this is a "do it" activity that involves the child in the preparation of the material, the means also become an end. The finished cards can be used as clue cards in finding the objects to fit into the figures at a later time. Or they can be used as a game of "object-rummy." However, the primary activity is the finger-hand movement made in the coloring by the child.

1. Have the child sit down at the table. Place the box of papers, 2 colored pencils, and the "saving can" on the table.

2. Take a piece of paper and 1 pencil and select 1 object from the group. Center the object on the paper and draw around its base, holding the paper with your nonwriting hand to keep it from moving. Return the object to the group.

3. Ask the child to make a selection and permit him to draw an outline.

4. On your own piece of paper, color in the outline with a different-colored pencil, using a natural movement (so as not to mislead the child into any labored movement). Be careful not to go outside the outline.

5. It is expected that the child will have picked up his pencil by now and will be attempting to fill in his figure.

6. This can be repeated with as many cards as the child likes, and for as many objects as he likes.

7. When he is finished, he can return the cards to the box, placing a rubber band around the completed ones and another around the unused ones. Return the objects either to the "saving can" or to their regular place in the household.

(Note: It is important that only one color be used at a time for each figure. However, the child can select a different color for a different object.)

Some Implications

In an age of nonstructured art, parents are often misled into believing that guiding the child in any way with writing or art materials will spoil his spontaneous use of such materials. Not all work with pencil, pen, or crayon is creative, however; some of it is done for the immediate pleasure of manipulating the material and exercising the hand, some for the feeling of mastery that comes with control of both the material and the body. It is for a combination of these reasons that we hope the child will do the activity and find satisfaction in it. Coloring books serve this purpose, too. However, there we see an unnecessary structuring of the images into pictures which can indeed thwart the child rather than satisfy or spur him on.

Since the child uses materials from the home he derives a double sense of pleasure—first, of recognition, and second, of finding his own objects to use later on. (This is the real test of success, even if the object is a favorite cup or vase!).

Both motor and eye coordination are needed to outline the objects, since some of them will have to be held in place. Skill in discerning and meeting this need will develop with experience.

Mastering the writing tool is difficult for many children. Fine hand muscles get much less developmental exercise than the larger muscles used in gross hand and arm movements. One way to utilize the small muscles between the ages of three to six is to use pencil, crayon, cray-pas, brush—using clay—and the fingers themselves.

Visual Discrimination: Size—Fine Hand Coordination

Materials

> 3 plastic cereal or dessert bowls
> 1 small plastic child-sized tray (obtainable in five and
>   ten cent stores, approximately 30 cents)
> Dried beans, rice, lentils, peas

Setup

1. Put the bowls on the tray.

2. Select 2 visually contrasting vegetables—rice and
    lentils, chick peas and lima beans, kidney beans
    and rice, dried peas and blackeyed beans.

3. Place a quarter of a cup of each in center bowl
    and mix them up.

Approach and Activity

This is a grand activity for a child when he is ill or when
he must be sedentary. It absorbs children for long periods
of time to the amazement of adults.

1. Take one pea or bean, etc., and place it in the
    child's hand. Let him get the feel of it, finger it,
    touch it, move it about.

2. Now take it away and let him do the same with
    a grain of rice or a lentil, etc.

3. Ask him to place into the left bowl, one piece at
    a time, all of the rice; into the right bowl, one
    piece at a time, the beans.

Some Implications

Getting children to pick up things is not always easy. But little fingers are in need of constant exercise in order to become the highly specialized manipulators they must be. While many everyday activities involve the child in such manipulation, activities that specifically coordinate the eye and the hand, as well as the fingers, are much rarer.

An interesting variation of this activity is to cover the child's eyes with a blindfold and let him divide the contents of a bowl by touch alone.

Visual Discrimination:
Size—Color

Materials

4 plastic bowls
10 or more 1-inch white buttons
10 or more 1-inch black buttons
10 or more ½-inch white buttons   } All of same design
10 or more ½-inch black buttons
Tray to hold all four bowls

Setup

A. 1. Three bowls on tray.

    2. Large black buttons and white buttons in middle bowl.

B. 1. Three bowls on tray.

    2. Small black buttons and white buttons in middle bowl.

C. 1. Three bowls on tray.

    2. Large and small white buttons or black buttons in middle bowl.

D. 1. Four bowls on tray.

    2. Buttons of both sizes and colors in lower right bowl.

Approach and Activity

This is a fourfold activity that involves the child in visual discrimination between objects. The procedure is exactly the same for the four activities, though the variable in each activity is different:

A. Color.
B. Color.
C. Size.
D. Color and Size.

   1. For A: Ask the child to choose one button and let him place it in the bowl on his right. Then let him take a button of the other color and put it into the bowl at his left. Repeat until the buttons are in the bowls. You can use "dark" and "light" or "black" and "white" to describe buttons.

   2. For B: Same procedure as A.

   3. For C: Since the buttons vary in size but not in color, say "large" and "small," "bigger," "smaller," etc., and proceed as in A.

   4. For D: Place D setup before child. Suggest that in each of the empty bowls (illustrate by doing) he place:

       small black buttons   small white buttons
       large black buttons   large white buttons

Some Implications

One of the interesting aspects in the development of thought in the child is his growing need to classify and label things. Few parents can meet the incessant demands

of a two- to three-year-old to name all things that come
into his view. By the time the child is three and four he is
already grouping things into classes: dogs, cats, tigers
equal *animals*; boys, girls, men, women, Mommy equal
people; parakeets, pigeons, canaries equal *birds*. This is a
significant period in the child's development because he is
beginning to put into order the world about him.

A manipulative activity requiring eye-hand coordination and finger dexterity as well as discrimination of
qualities is extremely absorbing to the child, so much so
that he will enjoy going back to it over and over again.

It is suggested that you do A, B, C, D in sequence,
one at a time; the sequence is developmental. However,
once the child has done each of these several times you
might leave the buttons, bowls, and tray on some
accessible shelf or table so that he can devise his own
activity.

Visual Discrimination:
Light Intensity—Color

Materials

> Liquid vegetable coloring
> Medium-sized clear pitcher
> Dozen or more jelly glasses, baby food jars or other
>   small jars
> A teaspoon
> A small sponge or piece of toweling
> Tray

Setup

Half-fill the pitcher with water. On the tray, place pitcher, glasses, spoon, sponge, and vegetable coloring in the three primary colors—red, yellow, and blue. Set the tray on a child-height table.

Approach and Activity

The purpose of this activity is to permit the child to create colors, and it is important that he be able to pour from a pitcher. This is a difficult task and the younger child may need pouring experience. (At bathtime, for example, plastic cups and bottles can be placed into the bath so that he can learn how to pour.) Get two creamers from the five-and-ten-cent store. Fill one with rice. Let the child pour rice from one creamer to the other. The spilt rice will also give him the opportunity to pick up very small objects with his fingers, a good finger-hand exercise. After several days, remove the rice and fill one of the creamers with some beach sand. It is advisable to set the creamers on a little tray or mat because the sand is more "liquid" in pouring than the rice. When the sand is spilled, the child will have to figure out how to get it back into the creamer. This is facilitated if the work area is limited.

When the child is able to hold a pitcher and pour with some ease, he is ready for his "color" activity. The tray helps to control spillage and, similarly, the sponge helps to manage any spilled water.

1. Take *one* bottle of the coloring from the container. (Caps generally show the color.) Have the child guess what color it is.

2. Have the child pour about 2 inches of water into four glasses.

3. Place a drop of coloring into the first glass. Observe the color change. Answer any questions, but do not ask any. This should not be a test situation.

4. Let him stir the contents with the spoon.

5. Now ask the child if he can make his own colored water in the next glass.

6. When this is done, ask him if he can make a darker color using the same glass. Let him answer by trying.

7. Ask him if he can make the water lighter.

8. Set these jars aside. Set out four more glasses. Have him fill them as before.

9. Let him select the next color from the container.

10. Unscrew the top. (This is usually too difficult for the child.)

11. Have him experiment with three of the glasses.

12. Suggest that he put a drop of his color into the fourth glass and you put in a drop of the first color.

13. Continue with at least one more color. Let his enthusiasm be the guide to how many colors are tried initially.

14. When the experimenting is over, place the glasses along a well-lighted windowsill so that the colors will look brighter. (If left for more than a few hours, the dye will separate from the water and float on the surface or sink. This separation is frequently very interesting for the child.)

Some Implications

For most of us, color is as important in our perception of things as line and shape. Many children can readily name the primary and secondary colors by the time they are four. Some have had experience in painting and mixing colors, generally in a nursery school situation. But every child should be able to explore and begin to form his own constructions related to color. Manipulation of color has a magical quality that greatly pleases the child. There is "magic" in the world we live in: one of man's greatest joys is beholding such magic. Color mixing holds many surprises. The child can actively manipulate the materials and observe the change. He can question himself and others. This learning by doing is perhaps the most fundamental and useful approach in thought devel-

opment. The child, on his own level, is structuring
scientific method. Much of what he observes in this
activity will be applied to other areas—painting, com-
menting on the world around him, translating color
intensity to mixture (thinning oatmeal, for example, by
adding more milk or water or thickening it by adding
more meal). It is this mental skill that is being sharpened.

There are physical gains, too. Control of the pitcher
means control of eye and hand movements, the same
control necessary later in writing. The experiencing of
weight through both the eye and the hand is another
valuable by-product.

One of the most interesting aspects of this activity is
the child's enthusiasm to create change. This can be
enhanced even further by the parent's active interest and
comments on such "marvels."

Visual Discrimination: Color

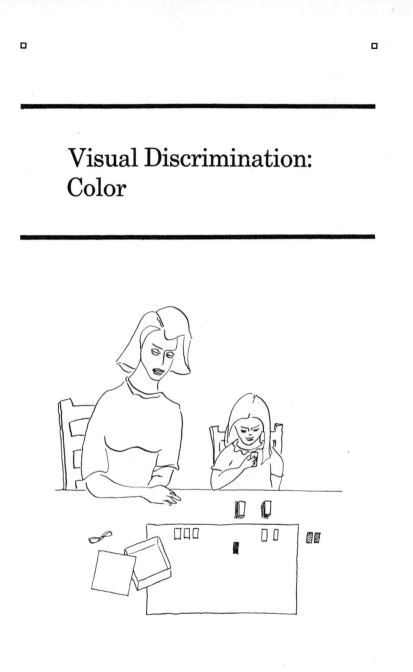

Materials

Paint chips from paint store—duplicates of each

Piece of white Contact-type paper

Small, plastic, rectangular see-through refrigerator container, such as single sandwich box

Piece of solidly colored cloth—a large napkin or regular place mat

Setup

1. Peel backing from part of the Contact and place paint chips (color side facing you) on the gummy backing of the paper.

2. Cut each chip and its backing from larger sheet. You will now have a double-thickness chip with one colored and one white side. (The printing found on the back of most chips will be covered by the Contact.)

3. Set the chips into two piles, making sure that a chip of each color is represented in each pile. Place rubber band about each pile and put them into the plastic container.

4. Set the napkin or place mat on a table with the container to one side.

5. Suggest that the child come and sit alongside you to play "color-rummy."

Approach and Activity

1. Open the container and place both piles in front of the child, below napkin or mat.

2. From one deck, deal out three cards to the child and three to yourself.

3. Now, each of you in turn take one card at a time from those remaining in the deck and attempt to match them to the cards in hand. When a match is made it should be laid out as "partners," ♠ ♠ at the winner's side. If a card does not match, it is returned to the bottom of the deck.

4. When the six matches are made, a winner is proclaimed and a decision is made whether to continue the game or not with other chips.

5. This game may also result in Solitaire follow-ups, trying to match one set to another.

Some Implications

Since paint chips come in a large variety of hues and intensities, the child has a splendid opportunity to discriminate the shades of a color. If the activity is enjoyable it can be varied as follows:

1. Use shades of green only.

2. Match the darkest shades of several colors.

3. Match the lightest shades of several colors.

4. Arrange chips according to hue value, lightest to darkest.

In this way the child refines his sense of color and practices visual discrimination.

Part of this activity requires a finger-hand manipulation of the comparatively small chips (1 inch by 1½ inches), so that small finger muscles will also be exercised.

Once started on the activity, both the parent and the child will enjoy finding ways to use these perceptions. A family game of hide-and-seek can be enjoyed by everyone. Set aside half a dozen or so chips. The person who is "it" picks a chip and tries to match it with something in the room (pattern on trays, book cover, lamp, etc., or everyone gets a chip and sets out to find its match. It is a good rule to preselect the chips so that success is assured.

Visual Discrimination:
Color II

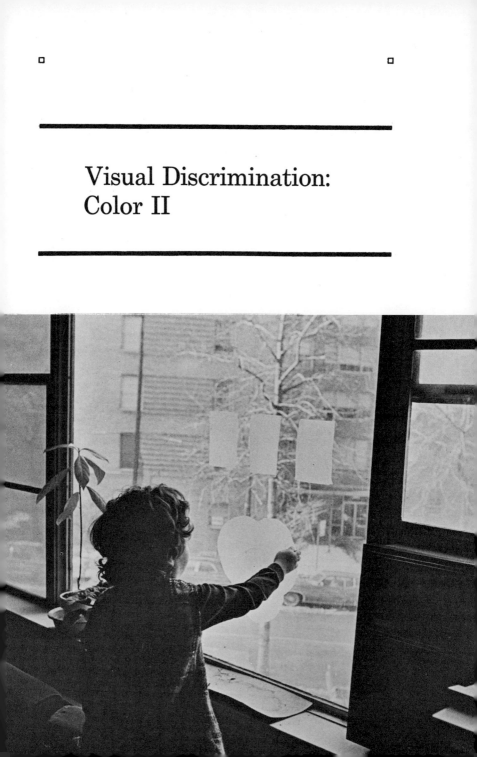

Materials

Scotch tape
Scissors
Package or roll of red, yellow, and blue cellophane

Setup

1. Cut from each color of cellophane a 3-inch by 6-inch strip.

2. Cut from each color cellophane a 5-inch diameter circle.

3. Select a window that gets sunlight during some part of the day.

4. Tape up strips on the window—one beneath the other.

5. Tape up circles on the window so that they overlap.

Approach and Activity

This is a long-term observation activity. It is meant to encourage curiosity about light and colors.

Call attention to the strips at various times of the day. The colors appear lighter and darker at different times. See how the sun heightens and intensifies the true color. What happened with the circles—are colors being formed by mixing? Does light also affect these newly created colors?

Some Implications

The importance of natural light to what we see is easily screened from our perceptions. Yet light has a magical power that intrigues us all. By setting up a color window for such casual observation, the child may be encouraged to create his own color window (made of pieces of cut cellophane taped to create free forms or realistic pictures or design), to look at stained-glass windows with some understanding of that art, and, largely, truly to see light as a life-giving force.

Visual Discrimination:
Color III

Materials

Cans from food closet

Setup

Have cans on easily reached shelves in closet or make a selection and put them in some interesting hiding place in the kitchen or a nearby area.

Look over the labels to familiarize yourself with the colors.

Approach and Activity

This is a hide-and-seek activity which has to be played by two. It is especially useful when a child is restless. It is important that this be a shared game rather than a demand-response activity.

Questions have to be carefully phrased: Can you find a can with a picture of a yellow vegetable? A Green Giant? A half red-half white label? A mostly red label? Dark blue letters that are larger than any others? Could a Green Giant be on any can we have? Is there a can that is half one color and half another?

Some Implications

Children today are veteran shoppers. They go along to the market, which is frequently part of their homelife through TV commercials. It is easy for them to identify by configuration. While this is an important skill, they may be screening out the colors they see by focusing on form. An activity such as this reintroduces color into these objects and affords both child and parent "talking" time within an explorative framework.

Also, since the cans are filled and are of various sizes, the activity permits hand and arm movements very like those involved in block building. Muscles in the fingers, and in the hand, wrist, and arm are all utilized, increasing the child's dexterity and adding to his awareness of what his body—and, therefore, his "self"—is capable of.

Tactile Sense

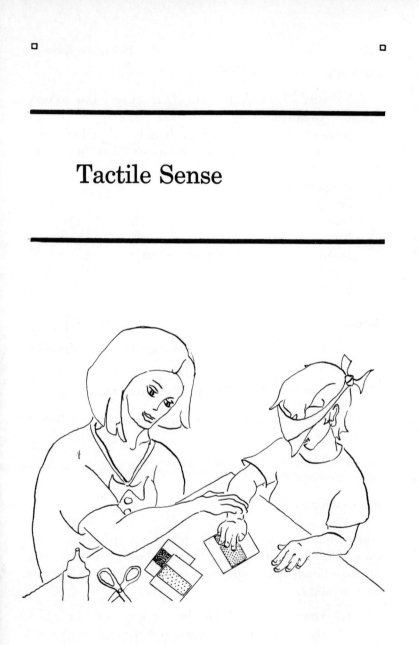

Materials

5 sheets of sandpaper ranging from very fine to very rough

A sheet of poster board, preferably colored (the size is usually 36 inches square or 24 inches by 30 inches)

2 board clips

Scissors

Sobo glue

Ruler

Small bowl (cereal) of warm water

Fingertip towel

Small bandana

Setup

1. Cut from each sheet of sandpaper two 3-inch by 1-inch strips.

2. Cut the poster board into 3-inch squares.

3. Paste sandpaper with rough side up across 3-inch squares (center).

4. Place in two matching piles, clip together.

Approach and Activity

Since this activity involves the sense of touch, the eyes—the immediate "touchers"—should be covered. Thus isolated, the fingers will be free to feel differences more acutely.

1. Have the child put his fingers into the warm water for a few minutes, as if using a finger bowl or having a manicure.

2. After each hand is dipped, let him dry it with the finger towel.

3. Set the bowl and towel to one side.

4. Take the bandana and make an eye mask so that the child cannot see, or else use a ready-made mask.

5. Select one card and place the child's hand on the smooth back side of the card. Let him stroke it lightly from left to right several times, with four fingers touching the board. Ask him to describe this.

6. Now turn the card over, place his fingers on the sandpaper (lightly). Let him repeat the stroking motion. Ask him to describe this.

7. Tell him that there are five cards that have "touch matches." Suggest that he touch each and try to find its match from second pile and to place those that match together. Set two piles in front of him.

Some Implications

Touching is a common activity of children. Many younger three- and four-year-olds still like to stroke anything smooth that comes their way. In this activity, therefore, the child not only gets pleasure, but also refines the discriminatory ability of his fingers. Children like to reaffirm their powers constantly. But much of a child's life today is textureless. The vast majority of objects in his room and in his home are made of plastics and wood. Not all children have the advantage of a vast outdoors filled with the textures of life. The home must therefore make some provision for satisfying the child's quest for texture as part of his broader quest for knowledge of all kinds.

Tactile Sense II

Materials

Mother, father, or any other obliging person
Blindfold

Setup

Quiet time activity which can be done while traveling, before or after naps, while child is restless during visits, etc.

Approach and Activity

This is a "touch game." The parent makes the rules, depending on the situation, it can be a sit-down activity, a come-and-find-me activity, etc.

1. Blindfold the child and perhaps yourself if you like. Tell him you are going to play a new kind of hide-and-seek. Instead of using people and your eyes, you are going to use things and find out what they are with your fingers.

2. Touch his cheek and say, "face" or "cheek" ("very smooth"), or touch his knee and say "knee" ("quite rough").

3. Let him touch you and identify both by name and by descriptive word: your dress ("smooth"); your belt ("stiff"); button ("hard"); stocking ("smooth"); shoes ("smooth" or "rough"); hair ("smooth" or "rough"); beard ("rough"); earlobes ("smooth"); nails ("hard"); tongue ("wet," "soft"); nose ("hard," "smooth").

4. Take turns trying to keep the child as interested as possible in only using his hand and fingers.

Some Implications

To preschoolers, their bodies and their parents' bodies serve as the warm blanket edge of security and known reality. How often does a toddler want to scramble up on a lap or back, happy in just touching body to body?

In Western civilization the body is a very personal manifestation of "I." As we grow, in fact, it becomes so much a psychological entity that we tend to accord it less and less substance as a contact point with the world. The human body, adorned for housework, beach, snow play, shopping, or visit is a veritable surprise box of textures and qualities. A child will take special delight in being able to relate physically to his parent and at the same time extend his physical pleasure to intellectual pleasure.

This kind of activity can also be done in a room or an apartment, or outdoors. A blindfold is not always needed indoors. You can give the child an assignment. "See if you can find something very rough. Touch it, and then come back and tell me what it is." It might be a rough drape, wood, rug, etc.

Tactile Sense III

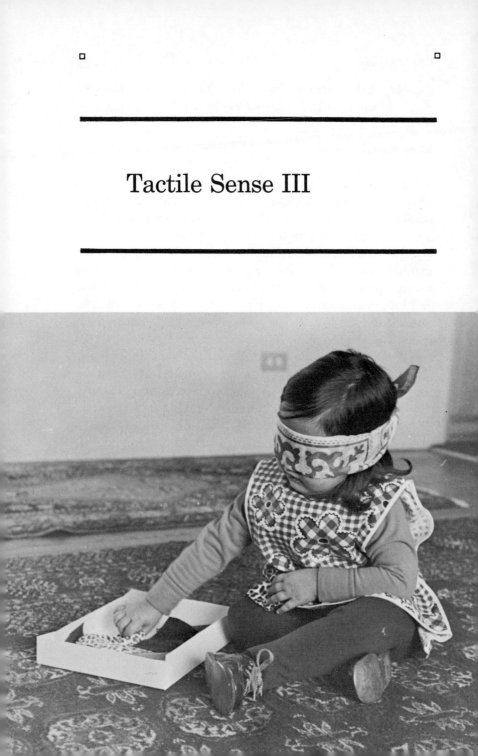

Materials

> Varieties of cloth—veiling, cottons of different
>   weights, silk, synthetics, wools, velvet, fake fur
> Flat box (for example, plastic sandwich box)
> Scissors (pinking shears, if possible)
> Blindfold

Setup

> Cut each type of cloth into 4-inch squares.
> Place in box.

Approach and Activity

The hands are the mediums of initial touch experience. The infant grasps things, fingers them, feels them. As he develops, he *senses* them to be objects rather than part of himself. Gradually he can use his eyes to discern objects. Yet the quality of touch in the use of the hand is important in terms of greater ability.

This activity requires the eyes to be covered in order to control the functioning of the eyes as "touchers."

This type of exercise has a threefold purpose: (1) discernment by contrast; (2) establishing identities; (3) enhance ability to perceive gradations in quality. The sequence is important.

Discernment by Contrast

1. Cover the child's eyes. Talk about his hands and fingers as "messengers."

2. Take sets of two very different textures—cotton and soft wool, silk and rough wool, veiling and

velvet—and let the child feel one then the other. Allow conversation to take place related to the "message." Use descriptive words such as smooth, rough, etc.

Establishing Identities

1. Once the child has experienced the contrasting identities, sort the swatches into two matching piles.

2. Blindfold him.

3. Give him a swatch, then ask him to find its match in the pile placed before him. When he feels that he has made a match, let him place both swatches together to one side.

4. Let him continue until he has matched all pieces.

5. When the job is done, uncover his eyes and let him visually check his matches and make any corrections or readjustments he wants.

Ability to Perceive Gradations

1. Take each complete set of the swatches and, at random, sort them into two separate piles.

2. Blindfold the child.

3. Ask him to place the swatches in order, ranging from smoothest to roughest or from lightest to heaviest.

4. Then ask him to find the matches from the second pile.

5. When the activity is over, have the child return the swatches to the box and return it to an accessible place.

Some Implications

Learning for many children is a highly personal experience. Yet in much of what we experience, significant learnings are often lost because of a diffusion in the activity itself. This specific threefold focusing of experience is a sound procedure for many sense learnings. In order to perceive differences from an experimental level, we must first "see" gross or contrasting difference (for example, rough and smooth). Then we can attempt to find similarities in other things so that classifications may be made and extended. Finally, with a highly "sensitized" tool—the hand or eye—we can make judgments in terms of degree or differences.

This type of doing is of basic value in much of our later thought. Reading, mathematics, language learning—all involve such procedural thinking. The senses and the organs involved in such "sensing" afford the child a pleasurable and significant means of such basic education.

Bibliography

Journals

Childhood Education. Association for Childhood Education International, 3615 Wisconsin Ave., N.W., Washington, D.C. 20016.

Children. United States Government Printing Office, Division of Documents, Washington, D.C. 20402.

Children's House. P.O. Box 111, Caldwell, N.J. 07006

Merrill-Palmer Quarterly of Behavior and Development. The Merrill-Palmer Institute, 71 East Ferry Ave., Detroit, Mich. 48202.

Young Children. National Association for the Education of Young Children, 1629 21 St., N.W., Washington, D.C. 20009.

Books for Children

Poetry

Herbert Read titled his collection of poetry, *This Way Delight.* For the child, poetry is indeed a source of constant delight. Pleasure in hearing the rhythm of words. Pleasure in feeling the impact of sounds. And pleasure in sensing a oneness with what is being thought.

The collection following ranges through early childhood, with a wide variety of paths that can be taken with young children. From "There was an old woman" to "I went out to the hazel wood," the child participates in the richness of life.

Behn, Harry, trans. *Cricket Song*(Japanese haiku). New York: Harcourt, Brace and World, Inc., 1964.

Brewton, John E. *Under the Tent of the Sky*. New York: The Macmillan Company, 1955.

Briggs, Raymond. *Fee-Fi-Fo-Fum.* New York: Coward-McCann, Inc., 1954.

_____. *Ring-A-Ring-O'Roses.* New York: Coward-McCann, Inc., 1962.

_____. *The White Land.* New York: Coward-McCann, Inc., 1963.

Brown, Margaret Wise. *Nibble, Nibble*. New York: William R. Scott, Inc., 1959.

Ciardi, John. *The Reason for the Pelican*. Philadelphia: J. B. Lippincott Company, 1959.

De la Mare, Walter. *Peacock Pie*. New York: Alfred A. Knopf, Inc., 1961.

Emberley, Barbara. *Drummer Hoff*. Englewood Cliffs, N.J.: Prentice-Hall, Inc., 1970.

Farjeon, Eleanor. *The Children's Bells*. New York: Henry Z. Walck, Inc., 1960.

Garnett, Eve. *A Book of the Seasons*. Cambridge, Mass.: Robert Bentley, Inc., 1961.

Issa, Yayu, and Kikaku. *Don't Tell the Scarecrow*. New York: Scholastic Book Services, 1969.

Lear, Edward. *The Complete Nonsense Book*. New York: Dodd, Mead and Company, 1962.

Lewis, Richard. *The Moment of Wonder*. New York: The Dial Press, Inc., 1964.

Lindsay, Vachel. *Johnny Appleseed and Other Poems*. New York: The Macmillan Company, 1964.

Milne, A. A. *The World of Christopher Robin*. New York: E. P. Dutton & Co., Inc., 1958.

Opie, Peter and Iona. *The Puffin Book of Nursery Rhymes.* Baltimore: Penguin Books, Inc., 1964.

Read, Herbert. *This Way Delight.* New York: Pantheon Books, Inc., 1957.

Reeves, James. *Ragged Robin.* New York: E. P. Dutton & Co., Inc., 1961.

Reeves, J. and others. *A Puffin Quartet of Poets.* Middlesex, England: Penguin Books, Ltd., 1958.

Rousseliere, Guy-Mary. *Beyond the High Hills: A Book of Eskimo Poems.* Cleveland: The World Publishing Company, 1961.

Sandburg, Carl. *Wind Song.* New York: Harcourt, Brace and World, Inc., 1953; paper, 1957.

Segal, Edythe. *Come with Me.* New York: Citadel Press, Inc., 1963.

Withers, Carl, and Jablow, Alba. *Rainbow in the Morning.* New York: Abelard-Schuman Limited, 1956.

Wyndham, Robert. *Chinese Mother Goose.* Cleveland: The World Publishing Company, 1968.

Music

There is growing evidence that children who have a good background in rhythm experiences, both with their bodies and voices, will have a much easier time learning to read. This selection includes books both for adults and children. The songs and activities are those of engagement. To paraphrase a popular song: Put a little music in your hearts and a great deal into your classrooms and homes.

Chappell, Warren. *Peter and the Wolf.* New York: Alfred A. Knopf, Inc., 1940.

———. *Hansel and Gretel.* New York: Alfred A. Knopf, Inc., 1944.

———. *The Nutcracker.* New York; Alfred A. Knopf, Inc., 1958.

Crowninshield, Ethel. *Stories That Sing.* Boston: The Boston Music Company, 1945.

Fisher, Edward. *The Animal Song Book.* New York: St. Martin's Press, Inc., 1962.

Gilmore, Lee. *Folk Instruments.* Minneapolis: Lerner Publications, 1964.

Hughes, Langston. *The First Book of Rhythms.* New York: Franklin Watts, Inc., 1954.

Jones, Harold. *Songs From Shakespeare.* Cranbury, N.J.: A. S. Barnes & Co., Inc., 1961.

Kapp, Paul. *A Cat Came Fiddling.* New York: Harcourt, Brace and Company, 1950.

Landeck, Beatrice. *Songs to Grow On.* New York: William Sloane Associates, Inc., 1956.

————. *More Songs to Grow On.* New York: William Sloane Associates, Inc., 1954.

Layton, Aviva. *The Singing Stones.* New York: Abelard-Schuman Limited, 1963.

Lear, Edward. *Nonsense Songs.* London: Frederick Warne & Co., Ltd., 1957.

Seeger, Ruth C. *American Folk Songs for Children.* New York: Doubleday & Company, Inc., 1948.

————. *Animal Folk Songs for Children.* New York: Doubleday & Company, Inc., 1950.

Spier, Peter. *The Fox Went Out on a Chilly Night.* New York: Scholastic Book Services, 1970.

Surplus, Robert W. *The Alphabet of Music.* Minneapolis: Lerner Publications, 1963.

Updike, John, and Chappell, W. *The King.* New York: Alfred A. Knopf, Inc., 1964.

————. *The Magic Flute.* New York: Alfred A. Knopf, Inc., 1963.

Von Schmidt, Eric. *Come for to Sing.* Boston: Houghton Mifflin Company, 1963.

Finger Plays

Grayson, Marion F. *Let's Do Finger Plays.* Washington, D.C.: Robert B. Luce, Inc., 1962.

Holl, Adelaide. *Finger Plays.* New York: Golden Press, 1964.

Jacobs, Francis S., *Finger Plays and Action Rhythms.* New York: Lothrop, Lee, 1941.

Owens, Ruby. *Musical Finger Plays.* 7225 Carmenita Rd., Lemon Grove, Calif. 92045, 1970.

Scott, Louise, and Thomson, J. T. *Rhymes for Fingers and Flannel Boards.* Manchester, Mo.: Webster Publishing Co., 1960.

Human Warmth

Harry Stack Sullivan postulated "the mothering one provides the basic pattern of being human or not human." There are certain books that call forth such intense warmth that children return to them over and over again. The books listed are a few that verify the child's sense of self and present an aesthetic quality that further enhances such feelings of worth.

Ets, Marie Hall. *Play With Me.* A Seafarer Book. The Viking Press, Inc., 1970.

Georgiou, Constantine. *Rani, Queen of the Jungle.* Englewood Cliffs, N.J.: Prentice-Hall, Inc., 1970.

Keeping, Charles. *Charley, Charlotte and the Golden Canary.* New York: Franklin Watts, Inc., 1967.

Lamorisse, Albert. *The Red Balloon.* Garden City, N.Y.: Doubleday & Company, Inc., 1956.

Leaf, Munro. *The Story of Ferdinand.* A Seafarer Book. New York: The Viking Press, Inc., 1970.

Levine, Rhoda. *Quiet Story.* New York: Atheneum Publishers, 1963.

Mariana. *The Journey of Bangwell Putt.* New York: Lothrop, Lee and Shepard Company, 1965.

Minarik, Else. *Little Bear.* New York: Harper & Bros., 1956.

Seuss, Dr. *Horton Hatches the Egg.* New York: Random House, Inc., 1940.

Stein, Gertrude. *The World Is Round.* New York: The Viking Press, Inc., 1972.

Swift, Hildegarde, and Ward, Lynd. *The Little Red Lighthouse.* New York: Harcourt, Brace and Company, 1942.

Ylla. *Animal Babies.* New York: Harper & Bros., 1959.

————. *The Little Elephant Baby.* New York: Harper & Bros., 1956.

Sounds and Imagery

While poetry deals with sounds and images, there are also certain works of fiction that provide particular richness. This is a short list, yet the vision of *I Can't Said the Ant* is of equal delight to that of *The Quiet Noisy Book*. The here-and-now information that children desire can be found in several of the nonfiction books listed.

Borten, Helen. *Do You Hear What I Hear?* New York: Abelard-Schuman Limited, 1959.

Brown, Margaret Wise. *SHHhhh . . . Bang.* New York: Harper & Bros., 1954.

_____ . *The Quiet Noisy Book.* New York: Harper & Bros., 1950.

Cameron, Polly. *I Can't Said the Ant.* New York: Scholastic Book Services, 1965.

deRegniers, Beatrice Schenk. *May I Bring a Friend?* New York: Atheneum Publishers, 1967.

Goudey, Alice. *The Day We Saw the Sun Come Up.* New York: Charles Scribner's Sons, 1961.

Krauss, Ruth. *Mama, I Wish I Was Snow; Child, You'd Be Very Cold.* New York: Atheneum Publishers, 1962.

McGovern, Ann. *Too Much Noise.* A See-Saw Book. New York: Scholastic Book Services, 1970.

Potter, Beatrix. *The Tailor of Gloucester.* London: Frederick Warne & Co., Ltd., 1903.

_____ . *The Tale of Benjamin Bunny.* London: Frederick Warne & Co., Ltd., 1904.

_____ . *The Tale of Mrs. Tittlemouse.* London: Frederick Warne & Co., Ltd., 1910.

_____ . *The Tale of Peter Rabbit.* London: Frederick Warne & Co., Ltd., 1904.

_____ . *The Tale of Squirrel Nutkin.* London: Frederick Warne & Co., Ltd., 1903.

Reid, Alastair. *Ounce Dice Trice.* Illus. by Ben Shahn. Boston: Little, Brown and Company, 1958.

Withers, Carl. *A Rocket in My Pocket.* New York: Henry Holt & Co., Inc., 1948.

Wolff, Janet. *Let's Imagine Sounds.* New York: E. P. Dutton & Co., Inc., 1964.

Visual Perception

In a sense modern man "sees," therefore, "he is." Yet so much of what is seen is not seen. There is a kaleidoscope quality to living that permits much to escape us. The books chosen for this section are of visual interest and quality. *Swimmy* moves through a living sea of great beauty. *Look Again* encourages one indeed to look again, perhaps even to think again. To touch with one's eyes offers all of us another way of perceiving and extending our ways of thinking.

Cameron, Polly. *The Boy Who Drew Birds.* New York: Coward-McCann, Inc., 1968.

Hoban, Tana. *Look Again.* New York: The Macmillan Company, 1971.

Lionni, Leo. *Swimmy.* New York: Pantheon Books, Inc., 1963.

MacAgy, Douglas and Elizabeth. *Going for a Walk with a Line.* Garden City, N.Y.: Doubleday & Company, Inc., 1959.

Selden, George. *I See What I See.* Farrar, Straus & Company, 1963.

Webber, Irma. *It Looks Like This.* A Point of View Book. New York: William R. Scott, Inc., 1949; New York: Scholastic Book Services, 1969.

Color

Gill, Bob. *From A to Z.* Boston: The Atlantic Monthly Press, 1962.

Keats, Ezra Jack. *Whistle for Willie.* A Seafarer Book. New York: The Viking Press, Inc., 1970.

Lionni, Leo. *Little Blue, Little Yellow.* New York: Ivan Obolensky, Inc., 1959.

Munari, Bruno. *A B C.* Cleveland: The World Publishing Company, 1960.

————. *Animals for Sale.* Cleveland: The World Publishing Company, 1957.

_____ . *Birthday Present.* Cleveland: The World Publishing Company, 1959.

_____ . *Elephant's Wish.* Cleveland: The World Publishing Company, 1959.

_____ . *Tic, Tac, and Toe.* Cleveland: The World Publishing Company, 1957.

_____ . *Who's There? Open the Door!* Cleveland: The World Publishing Company, 1957.

_____ . *Zoo.* Cleveland: The World Publishing Company, 1963.

Piatti, Celestine. *The Happy Owls.* New York: Atheneum Publishers, 1964.

Surany, Anico. *Ride the Cold Wind.* New York: G. P. Putnam's Sons, 1964.

Wolff, Janet. *Let's Imagine Colors.* New York: E. P. Dutton & Co., Inc., 1963.

Young, Mary. *Singing Windows.* Nashville, Tenn.: Abingdon Press, 1962.

Form

Downer, Marion. *The Story of Design.* New York: Lothrop, Lee & Shepard Company, Inc., 1963.

Glubock, Shirley. *The Art of the Eskimo.* New York: Harper & Row, Publishers, 1964.

_____ . *Art of the North American Indian.* New York: Harper & Row, Publishers, 1964.

Hughes, Peter. *The Emperor's Oblong Pancake.* New York: Abelard-Schuman Limited, 1961.

deRegniers, Beatrice Schenk. *The Shadow Book.* Harcourt, Brace and Company, 1960.

Schlein, Miriam. *Shapes.* New York: William R. Scott, Inc., 1952.

Size

Berkley, Ethel. *The Size of It.* New York: William R. Scott, Inc., 1960.

Cook, Bernadine. *The Little Fish That Got Away.* New York: Scholastic Book Services, 1965.

Crowell, Volrey. *How to Hide a Hippopotamus.* New York: Dodd, Mead & Company, 1958.

Ga'g, Wanda. *Nothing at All.* New York: Coward-McCann, Inc., 1941.

Lenski, Lois. *Cowboy Small.* New York: Henry Z. Walck, Inc., 1949.

_____ . *The Little Airplane.* New York: Henry Z. Walck, Inc., 1938.

_____ . *The Little Auto.* New York: Henry Z. Walck, Inc., 1934.

_____ . *The Little Farm.* New York: Henry Z. Walck, Inc., 1942.

_____ . *The Little Fire Engine.* New York: Henry Z. Walck, Inc., 1946.

Titus, Eve. *The Mouse and the Lion.* New York: Parents' Magazine Press, 1962.

Whipple, Dorothy. *The Smallest Tortoise of All.* London: Frederick Warne & Co., Ltd., 1962.

Time and Space

Growth means movement in time and space. Fortunately, there is a vast resource to be found in children's books to help us, child and adult, position ourselves in time and space.

The books chosen for inclusion include fiction, poetry, and nonfiction. These books can help dispel the tiny tremors of terror that growing holds for all of us.

Day and Night

Belting, Natalie. *The Sun Is a Golden Earring* (poetry). New York: Holt, Rinehart and Winston, Inc., 1962.

Branley, Franklyn. *The Moon Seems to Change.* New York: Thomas Y. Crowell Company, 1960.

Brown, N. W. *Goodnight Moon.* New York: Scholastic Book Services, 1970.

Burton, Virginia Lee. *Mike Mulligan and His Steam Shovel.* Boston: Houghton Mifflin Company, 1939.

Flack, Marjorie. *The Story About Ping.* A Seafarer Book. New York: The Viking Press, Inc., 1969.

Scarry, Richard. *The Early Bird.* New York: Random House, Inc., 1968.

Thurber, James. *Many Moons.* New York: Harcourt, Brace and Company, 1943.

Seasons

Belting, Natalie. *Calendar Moon.* New York: Holt, Rinehart and Winston, Inc., 1964.

Birnbaum, A. *Green Eyes.* New York: Capitol Publishing Company, 1953.

Branley, Franklyn. *Snow Is Falling.* New York: Thomas Y. Crowell Company, 1963.

Brown, Margaret Wise, and Gergely, Tibor. *Wheel on the Chimney.* Philadelphia: J. B. Lippincott Company, 1954.

Buff, Mary. *Forest Folk.* New York: The Viking Press, Inc., 1962.

Floathe, Louise Lee. *Blueberry Pie.* New York: Charles Scribner's Sons, 1962.

Frasconi, Antonio. *The Snow and the Sun.* New York: Harcourt, Brace & World, Inc., 1961.

Goudey, Alice. *Butterfly Time.* New York: Charles Scribner's Sons, 1964.

Hader, Berta and Elmer. *The Big Snow.* New York: The Macmillan Company, 1948.

McDonald, Golden (pseudonym for Margaret Wise Brown), and Weisgard, Leonard. *The Little Island.* New York: Doubleday & Company, Inc., 1946.

Radlauer, Ruth. *About Four Seasons and Five Senses.* Chicago: Melmont Publishers, Inc., 1960.

Tresselt, Alvin. *Autumn Harvest.* New York: Lothrop, Lee & Shepard Company, Inc., 1960.

Zolotow, Charlotte. *The Storm Book.* New York: Harper & Bros., 1952.

Passage of Time

Asinov, Isaac. *The Clock We Live On.* New York: Abelard-Schuman Limited, 1959.

Françoise. *What Time Is It, Jeanne-Marie?* New York: Charles Scribner's Sons, 1963.

Kirkpatrick, Leonard N. *How Old Are You?* New York: Abelard-Schuman Limited, 1962.

Schlein, Miriam. *It's About Time.* New York: William R. Scott, Inc., 1955.

Sendak, Maurice. *Where the Wild Things Are.* New York: Scholastic Book Services, 1970.

Slobodkina, Esphyr. *The Clock.* New York: Abelard-Schuman Limited, 1956.

Smith, Robert Paul. *When I Am Big.* New York: Harper & Row, Publishers, 1965.

Direction

Webber, Irma. *Up Above and Down Below.* New York: William R. Scott, Inc., 1943.

Zion, Gene. *All Falling Down.* New York: Harper & Row, Publishers, 1951.

Movement

Borten, Helen. *Do You Move as I Do?* New York: Abelard-Schuman Limited, 1963.

Ets, Mary Hall. *Gilberto and the Wind.* A Seafarer Book. New York: The Viking Press, Inc., 1967.

Woodcock, L. *This Is the Way Animals Walk.* Eau Claire, Wis.: E. M. Hale & Company, 1964.

The World About Us

Adults are steeped in the problems of today: pollution, advanced technology, overpopulation, wars. The list is endless and the anxieties created are infinite in effect. Literature has always served man as a means to understand his world further. Children's literature can also greatly help the child to understand his world. These books reflect wonder, awareness, beauty, and knowledge. They can help you make the world more comprehensible to your child.

Beskow, Elsa. *Pelle's New Suit.* New York: Harper & Bros., 1961.

Brown, Margaret Wise. *The Important Book.* New York: Harper & Bros., 1949.

Darbois, Dominique. *Agossou: The Little African.* Paris: Nathan, 1955.

Hodges, Margaret. *The Wave.* Boston: Houghton Mifflin Company, 1964.

Mace, Katherine. *A Tail Is a Tail.* New York: Abelard-Schuman Limited. 1957.

Neurath, Marie. *Building Big Things.* London: Max Parrish, 1958.

Paull, Grace. *Come to the Country.* New York: Abelard-Schuman Limited, 1956.

_____ . *Some Day.* New York: Abelard-Schuman Limited, 1957.

Rose, Elizabeth and Gerald. *The Big River.* London: Faber and Faber, 1962.

Sucksdorff, A. B., and Sansom, William. *Chendru: The Boy and the Tiger.* London: Collins, 1960.

Wolff, Janet. *Let's Imagine Going Places.* New York: E. P. Dutton & Co., Inc., 1961.

Nature

Clark, Ann Nolan. *Tia Maria's Garden.* New York: The Viking Press, Inc., 1963.

Collier, Ethel. *Who Goes There in My Garden?* Reading, Mass.: Young Scott Books, 1963.

Cooke, Emogene. *Funtime Garden.* Chicago: Children's Press, 1951.

Graham, Margaret. *Be Nice to Spiders.* New York: Harper & Row, Publishers, 1967.

Lubell, Winifred and Cecil. *Green Is for Growing.* Chicago: Rand McNally & Company, 1963.

McCaffery, Janet R. *The Swamp Witch.* New York: William Morrow and Company, 1970.

Reidman, Sarah. *Naming Living Things.* Chicago: Rand McNally & Company, 1963.

Rothschild, Alice. *Fruit Is Ripe for Timothy.* New York: William R. Scott, Inc., 1963.

Stevens, Carla. *Catch a Cricket.* Reading, Mass.: Young Scott Books, 1961.

Tressett, Alvin. *Raindrop Splash*. New York: Lothrop, Lee & Shepard Company, Inc., 1952.

Numerical Concepts

Books related to numbers can be found in ever-increasing number. The few books chosen reflect a strong aesthetic quality that integrates numbers rather than isolates them. As children experience numerical concepts, e.g., *Jeanne-Marie Counts Her Sheep* or *Millions of Cats*, they become more interested in the relevancy of the concepts and can see them as part of their own interest and lives.

Cooke, Barbara. *My Daddy and I*. New York: Abelard-Schuman Limited, 1963.

Doisneau, Roger, and Gregor, Arthur. *1 2 3 4 5*. Philadelphia: J. B. Lippincott Company, 1956.

Françoise. *Jeanne-Marie Counts Her Sheep*. New York: Charles Scribner's Sons, 1951.

Ga'g, W. *Millions of Cats*. New York: Coward-McCann, Inc., 1928.

Slobodkina, Esphyr. *Caps for Sale*. New York: Scholastic Book Services, 1969.

Tudor, Tasha. *1 Is One*. New York: Oxford University Press, Inc., 1956.

Sensory Activity

For the very young child these books can provide many pleasurable experiences. If they are read by the adult in a spirit of warmth and sharing, the child can touch, feel, and even smell while hearing words that carry immediate meaning to him.

Brown, Margaret Wise. *Young Kangaroo*. New York: William R. Scott, Inc., 1955.

Kunhardt, Dorothy. *Pat the Bunny*. New York: Golden Books, 1940.

Witte, Pat and Eve. *The Touch Me Book*. New York: Capitol Publishing Company, 1961.

Records

Stories

Horton Hatches the Egg. MGM, Leo 1013.

> A first-rate rendering of a charming story filled with justice from a child's point of view.

The House at Pooh Corner and Now We Are Six. Golden, GW 228.

> This stands up and out as the most listened to of the many Pooh records. The music is superb.

The Tale of Benjamin Bunny. Vivien Leigh. Golden, GW 227.

> An interesting sequel to Peter Rabbit.

The Tale of Jemima Puddleduck. Vivien Leigh. Golden, GW 224.

> Delightful listening; words and music hold the attention of young children.

The Tale of Peter Rabbit. Vivien Leigh. Golden, GW 210.

> The story is charmingly told and the music is of excellent quality.

The Wizard of Oz. Judy Garland. MGM, PX #104, stereo.

> A classic for the four- to six-year-old.

Uncle Wiggly and His Friends. RCA Camden, 5-1116.

> Delightful tales filled with the incongruous.

Songs for Listening and Singing

American Folk Songs for Children. Pete Seeger. Folkways, 7001, 10-inch.

> Crisp, charming collection.

The Baby Sitters' Family Album. Vanguard, VRS 9173.

> Another album filled with pleasure from the Baby Sitters.

Burl Ives Sings for Fun. Decca, DL 8248.

Lively, manly sounds.

Children's Songs. Johnny Richardson. Folkways, FC 7678.

A strong masculine voice with such favorites as "Katy-the-Kangaroo" and "Six Little Mice."

Folk Songs for Babies, Small Children, Baby Sitters and Parents. The Baby Sitters. Vanguard, VRS 9046.

One of the finest listening and loving records for the family.

Golden Slumber: Lullabies from Near and Far. Caedmon I.

An unusual combination of beauty-text, artwork, music, and record for family sharing.

Menagerie. Baby Sitters. Vanguard, 79288.

Animals galore in this tuneful record.

Pete Seeger Sings: Folk Songs for Young People. Folkways, 7532.

A very good basic collection.

Sleep-time: Songs and Stories. Pete Seeger. Folkways, 7525.

Good rest-time sounds.

Songs to Grow On: Varied Voices and Instruments. Vol. 2. Folkways, 7020.

An interesting grouping. Lyrices and music can be found in Beatrice Landeck's book.

Songs for the Wee Folk. Susan Reed. Electra, 163.

A splendid voice with beautiful material.

Susan Reed. Electra, 116.

English and Spanish folk songs for quiet times.

A Treasury of Spanish-Mexican Folk Songs. Cynthia Gooding. Electra, 218.

Lovely songs for quiet times (in Spanish).

You Can Sing It Yourself. Robin Christenson. Folkways, 7624 A.

First-rate collection.

Songs for Learning

Counting Games and Rhythms for the Little Ones. Ella Jenkins. Folkways, 7056.

Sounds of children playing together are most supportive.

More Learning as We Play. Folkways, 7658.

"Songs, rhythms—beginning rhythm band activities."

Mother Goose and Father Gander. Cynthia Gooding and Don Drake. RCA Camden, 1058.

An extraordinary delight for the ear.

Song and Play-time. Pete Seeger. Folkways, 7526.

Music and words for many games.

Music for Movement

Beethoven Violin Concerto in D Major. David Oistrakh. Angel, 35162.

A Must for babes and parents to soothe and salvage.

By Rocket to the Moon. Young People's Records, YPR 15016.

Filled with the sounds and spirit of space travel; especially good for dramatic play.

Byrd Land. Charlie Byrd. Columbia, CL 2592.

A guitar at its best; interesting for group improvisations.

Chopin—14 Waltzes. Alexander Brailowsky, pianist. Phillips, ABC 3311.

Boys and girls respond to this music; very useful for improvisations.

Flute Concertos by Bach and Telemann. Jean-Pierre Rampal. Epic, LC 3921.

Children respond to this music with their bodies in space.

Improvisations for Modern Dance. Sarah Malament. 3215 Netherland Ave., New York, N.Y. 10063.

Especially useful with small groups. Strong piano direction.

Jazz Loves Bach. The Wayland Quartet. Kapp, FCS 4249.

For rainy days; useful for improvisations.

Keep Fit—Be Happy. Bonnie Prudden. Warner Bros., WS 1358.

Exercises for fun and health. Pictures and music for the whole family.

The Little Fireman. Margaret Wise Brown. Young People's Records, 10003.

A delightful rendering of this popular book; good for dramatic play.

Me, Myself and I, My Playful Scarf. Young People's Records, 10012.

Lovely for dramatic play and movement.

Mendelssohn: A Midsummer Night's Dream; Humperdinck: Hansel and Gretel. Seraphim, 60056.

Either side will gather a group of children.

Mozart—The Complete Flute Sonatas. Jean-Pierre Rampal, flutist. Epic, LC 3888.

For listening or body movement; a joy.

Scheherazade. Vienna State Orchestra. Vanguard, SRV 163 SD.

A fine record for getting children to move and listen.

Tchaikowsky: Album for the Young, Op. 39. Ania Dorfman, pianist. RCA Victor, IM 1856.

A beautiful, lively collection for body-movement work.

Books for Adults

Development

Ariès, Philippe. *Centuries of Childhood.* A Vintage Book. New York: Random House, Inc., 1962.

For those interested in historical backgrounds this book is a social history of family life.

Fraiberg, Selma. *The Magic Years.* New York: Charles Scribner's Sons, 1969.

A tidy and useful guide for parents and those entrusted with the care of young children.

Gesell, Arnold. *Infant and Child in the Culture of Today.* New York: Harper & Row, Publishers, 1943.

An early work of value for parents of young children. Psychology of development is graphically presented.

Ilg, F., and Ames, L. *Child Behavior.* A Perennial Book. New York: Harper & Row, Publishers, 1966.

A handbook for every parent and day-care worker. Concise, timely, and useful information of immediate value.

Lichtenberg, P., and Norton, Dolores. *Cognitive and Mental Development in the First Five Years of Life.* Chevy Chase, Md.: NIMH, 1970.

A review of recent research in the areas of play, language, cognitive development, and functioning. Role of the parent in such development is of special interest.

Millar, Susanna. *The Psychology of Play.* Baltimore: Penguin Books, Inc., 1969.

A definite and readable text on "play." Highly recommended for teachers and interested parents.

Montessori, Maria. *What You Should Know About Your Child.* Madras, India: Kalakshetra Publ., 1961.

A series of lectures for those interested in alternate ways of seeing the young child.

_____ . *The Child in the Family: A Manifesto for Parents.* New York: Avon Books, 1970.

This book will provide many questions for parents and all those who work with the young child.

Newson, John and Elizabeth. *Patterns of Infant Care.* Baltimore: Penguin Books, Inc., 1963.

A sociological study of infant care in an urban community in Great Britain. Of special interest to day-care personnel.

Pickard, P. M. *Psychology of Developing Children.* London: Longman Group Ltd., 1970.

Comprehensive and readable up-to-date (language, play, exceptional children) information on the developing child. Research studies cited would be of particular interest for college students and teachers.

Sullivan, H. S. *The Interpersonal Theory of Psychiatry.* New York: W. W. Norton & Company, Inc., 1970.

A technical book; of great value to those with a strong psychology background.

Valentine, C. W. *The Normal Child.* Middlesex, England: Penguin Books, Ltd., 1956.

One of the most readable guides to the behavior of children with particular attention to those actions that are frequently mistaken as abnormalities. A must for workers and parents.

Wadsworth, Barry T. *Piaget's Theory of Cognitive Development.* New York: David McKay Co., Inc., 1971.

A most readable Piaget guide. Can serve students, teachers, and parents as a means of seeing children develop.

Wagenknecht, Edward. *When I Was a Child.* New York: E. P. Dutton & Co., Inc., 1946.

A delightful anthology of childhood remembrances.

Winnicott, D. W. *The Child, the Family, and the Outside World.* Middlesex, England: Penguin Books, Ltd., 1969.

A comprehensive and useful book on mothering. Valuable for parents and those who work with parents.

Yamamoto, Kaoru, ed. *The Child and His Image; Self Concept in the Early Years.* Boston: Houghton Mifflin Company, 1972.

A timely book for those involved with helping children grow.

Language

Brogan, Peggy, and Fox, L. *Helping Children Read.* New York: Holt, Rinehart and Winston, Inc., 1961.

Teachers of five- and six-year-olds will appreciate this practical and informative text.

Child Study Association of America. *The Children's Bookshelf.* New York: Bantam Books, 1962.

A parents' guide to good books. Most useful for those selecting books.

Chukovsky, Kornei. *From Two to Five.* Berkeley, Calif.: University of California Press, 1963.

Language in its beauty, use, and pleasure is explored through children. The work of a Russian poet and author of children's books is a must for all those interested in the language of the young child.

Foster, Joanna. *How to Conduct Effective Picture Book Programs.* New York: Westchester Library System, 1967.

Useful and interesting guide for use with very young children and books.

Gardner, Keith. *Towards Literacy.* Oxford, England: Basil Blackwell & Mott, Ltd., 1967.

A very small book that is an excellent guide toward an examination of the nature of reading, the purposes of reading, and "the relation of reading to the complex mental development of young children."

Georgiou, Constantine. *Children and Their Literature.* Englewood Cliffs, N.J.: Prentice-Hall, 1967.

An excellent guide to children and books for teachers and interested parents.

Jennings, Frank. *This Is Reading.* A Delta Book. New York: Dell Publishing Co., 1966.

Reading put into perspective. This is a book that should be read by all parents.

Sapir, Edward. *Language.* New York: Harcourt, Brace & World, Inc., 1921.

An introduction to the study of speech by one of the country's greatest linguists. Of historical and practical value to the student of speech and language development.

Vygotsky, Lev. *Thought and Language.* Cambridge, Mass.: MIT Press, 1962.

Theoretical presentation of immense value to any student of mental development. An extraordinary work.

Movement

Bentley, William. *Learning to Move and Moving to Learn.* New York: Scholastic Book Services, 1970.

Concise and inexpensive manual for use with children in small groups at school.

Cameron, W., and Pleasant, P. *Education in Movement.* Oxford, England: Basil Blackwell & Mott, Ltd., 1969.

Of special interest to those who work with small groups of children. Applied techniques of Rudolph Laban.

Cherry, Clare. *Creative Movement for the Developing Child.* Palo Alto, Calif.: Fearon Publ., 1968.

Splendid handbook for those who work with preschool children in day-care centers and nurseries.

Hatcher, C., and Mullin, Hilda. *More Than Words.* Pasadena, Calif.: Parents-for-Movement, 1967.

Movement activities for children in the home and in small groups. Very thoughtful.

Jordan, Diana. *Childhood and Movement.* Oxford, England: Basil Blackwell & Mott, Ltd., 1966.

A primer for those interested in the work of Rudolph Laban. Beautiful introduction to movement as development in the young child. Directed to teachers, of interest to parents.

Prudden, Bonnie. *How to Keep Your Child Fit from Birth to Six.* New York: Harper & Row, Publishers, 1964.

An invaluable guide for parents and teachers.

Art

Bland, Jane Cooper. *Art of the Young Child.* New York: The Museum of Modern Art, 1957.

A guide of value and interest. Well-presented pictures and text by one who has worked with children and their parents.

Dunnett, Ruth. *Art and Child Personality.* New York: British Book Centre, 1948.

An account of a group of boys' experiences with art—boys with adjustment problems.

Johnson, Harriet. *The Art of Blockbuilding.* New York: Bank Street Publications, 1966.

Classic study of blocks, block building, and children as they build with blocks. Parents, students, and teachers will find this of great value.

Lindstrom, Miriam. *Children's Art.* Berkeley, Calif.: University of California Press, 1959.

With text and illustrations, the author has provided an excellent basis for seeing the young child and his art.

Montgomery, Chandler. *Art for Teachers of Children.* Columbus, Ohio: Charles E. Merrill Publishing Company, 1968.

For all interested in aesthetic development. Most readable, most usable.

Saunders, Everett. *Paper Art Constructing Painting.* Racine, Wis.: Whitman Publishing Company, 1966.

A series of practical use in providing act activities for children.

Starks, Esther B. *Blockbuilding.* Washington, D.C.: American Association of Elementary-Kindergarten-Nursery Educators, NEA Center, 1970.

A block-building primer. Especially useful for those who live and work with four- and five-year-olds.

Learning

Beyer, Evelyn. *Teaching Young Children.* A Pegasus Book. New York: The Bobbs-Merrill Co., Inc., 1968.

A comfortable book for those who would like to familiarize themselves with nursery education.

Brearley, Molly, ed. *The Teaching of Young Children.* New York: Schocken Books, 1970.

The subtitle of this book is "Some Applications of Piaget's Learning Theory." A guide for teachers, especially in the areas of music, movement, language, and art.

Chauncey, Henry, ed. *Soviet Pre-School Education.* New York: Holt, Rinehart and Winston, Inc., 1969.

An interesting addition to comparative studies of educating young children.

Clure, Beth. *Why Didn't I Think of That?* Glendale, Calif.: Bowmac, 1971.

A very crisp, useful resource book. Good for beginning teachers.

Infant Care Project Progress Report. Greensboro, N.C.: University of North Carolina, 1971.

Some aids for those working with infants and toddlers.

Montessori, Maria. *The Discovery of the Child.* New York: Ballantine Books, Inc., 1972; Madras, India: Kalakshetra Publ., 1962.

Both editions of this book are translations; however, the Indian edition was jointly done by Maria Montessori and Mary

Johnstone. This book is the final synthesis of a number of earlier works by Maria Montessori. A must for all those interested in the development of Montessorian theory.

Orem, R. C. *Montessori and the Special Child.* New York: G. P. Putnam's Sons, 1970.

A collection centered about the application of Montessori principles. Of special interest to parents and teachers of children who are not mainstream normal.

Services

Sources for Tapes, Cassettes, Records, Supplies

Bowman
622 Rodier Drive
Glendale, Calif. 91201

Catalog of material of special
  interest:
Bilingual education
Early childhood
Physical education
Special education

Childhood Resources, Inc.
1150 Connecticut Ave., N.W.
Washington, D.C. 20036

Tape-of-the-Month in Early
  Childhood

Lyons, Dept. N
430 Wrightwood Ave.
Elmhurst, Ill. 60126

Excellent catalog
Body-movement records
Music materials

Mead Educational Services
245 N. Highland Ave., N.E.
Atlanta, Ga. 30307

Early childhood learning tools
  catalog.

Miller Brody Productions, Inc.
Audio-Visual Instructional
    Programs
324 Madison Ave.
New York, N.Y. 10017

1. The Early Learning
   Filmstrip Library
2. Pick a Peck O' Poems
3. The Newbery Award
   Records, Cassettes and
   Filmstrips
4. Bilingual Records and
   Cassettes

A most interesting catalog;
materials for both home and
school use.

J. A. Preston Corp.
71 Fifth Ave.
New York, N.Y. 10003

Catalog of materials for
exceptional children and
youth.

PRL—Educational Aids &
    Materials
36 Hillside Ave.
Williston Park, L.I., N.Y.
    11596

Taskmaster Aids (Leicester-
shire Math Apparatus) and
other early-learning
materials.

Radiant Corp.
Knowledge Aid Division
Norton Grove, Ill. 60053

Cassette catalog of wide range.

Schwann Catalogue, Children's
    Records
137 Newburg St.
Boston, Mass. 02116

Up-to-date catalog of records
available commercially.

See-Saw Books
Scholastic Book Services
904 Sylvan Ave.
Englewood Cliffs, N.J. 07632

Books and records for the
preschooler.

Sources for Film Catalogs

Anti-Defamation League of B'nai B'rith
315 Lexington Ave.
New York, N.Y. 10016

British Broadcasting Corporation
230 Park Ave.
New York, N.Y. 10017

Center for Media Development, Inc.
Box 203
Little Neck, L.I., N.Y. 11363

Education Development Center, Inc.
55 Chapel St.
Newton, Mass. 02160

Far West Regional Laboratory
Hotel Claremont
Berkeley, Calif. 94705

International Film Bureau
332 S. Michigan Ave.
Chicago, Ill. 60604

National Council of Churches
Department of Visual Education
475 Riverside Dr.
New York, N.Y. 10024

National Film Board of Canada
680 Fifth Ave.
New York, N.Y. 10019

New York University Film Library
26 Washington Pl.
New York, N.Y. 10003

OEO Film Guide (1967)
U.S. Government Printing Office
Washington, D.C. 20401

University of California, Media Center
2233 Fulton St.
Berkeley, Calif. 94720

Washington Montessori Institute
2119 S St., N.W.
Washington, D.C. 20008

Index